Z-80 and 8080
Assembly Language
Programming

Hayden Computer Programming Series

Z-8Ø and 8Ø8Ø Assembly Language Programming

KATHE SPRACKLEN

HAYDEN BOOK COMPANY, INC.
Rochelle Park, New Jersey

To my precious stepdaughters
Teresa and Amy

ISBN 0-8104-5167-0
Library of Congress Catalog Card Number 79-65355

7   8   9   PRINTING

82 83 84 85 86 87   YEAR

Preface

My first concern was chess. The dream was and is to create a microcomputer program that can play chess at the master level. But computer chess could not be done effectively using BASIC. It had to be assembly language. For Dan and me learning and using Z-80 assembly language posed no problem because of our prior background writing in other assembly level languages. But we wanted also to share what we had done in creating SARGON, and for many potentially gifted programmers there seemed to be a desperate lack of suitable introductory material. I was especially concerned with texts that insult the intelligence of the reader. Yet among those written for the capable layman there seemed to be a heavy emphasis on the hardware aspects of microprocessors. What I wanted to see was a book that taught Z-80 assembly language as a *first* assembly language; a book that emphasized *software* and covered the *uses* of the machine instructions in tackling a programming project. This book was written to fill that need.

In creating this book I owe a double debt to Professor David Solomon, San Diego State University. Dr. Solomon provided me with my first introduction to assembly language and later to microcomputers. In his classes I enjoyed the delicious dawning of understanding of just what a computer is and does. I thank my students at The Computer Center, Ronson Rd., San Diego, for their comments and suggestions on the first draft of this book, particularly Arthur Wolman. To my husband, Dan, go many thanks for giving me the computer "bug" in the first place and for leading the way in computer chess. Finally I would like to thank my mother, Margaret Shannon, and my grandmother, Julia Dumas, for providing two generations of creative, competent women to admire and emulate.

KATHE SPRACKLEN

San Diego

Contents

introduction

Are you bored with BASIC?

Do your photon torpedoes drift listlessly across your screen?

Does it take ages to age your accounts receivable?

Maybe you're ready to tackle assembly language programming. If so, this is the place to start. This book assumes that you know a little bit about computers and have done some programming in a higher level language like BASIC or FORTRAN. It assumes familiarity with words like

VARIABLE
GOTO
LOOP
ARRAY

The approach is designed for the novice to assembly programming and is intended to provide just about everything the applications programmer needs to know to get the most out of his machine. Some topics are conspicuously omitted, since they are really relevant only to someone designing a monitor program or operating system. The emphasis here is to give the user all the information needed to interact with his monitor.

Here are some of the features that make this book unique.

- Each concept and instruction is carefully explained.
- Numerous diagrams and examples are provided.
- Exercises designed to instruct and challenge you are included with each chapter, and answers to each are provided.
- Programming techniques are presented along with the instructions.

There are eight chapters in this book. Each chapter gradually builds on the work of preceding ones. The exercises are a part of the instructional material as well. Do try them. They will help you quickly develop your skills as an assembly language programmer, as most exercises ask you to write segments of code. When you turn to the answers, however, please remember that what you see is but one possible way of doing things. It is very unlikely that we will

1

agree totally on the approach to take, so to check your work try it out on your computer.

Assembly programming is really worth the effort it takes when you're new at it. Later, when you become comfortable with the instructions, it is only slightly more difficult than BASIC. In return it gives you

- complete control of your system
- flexibility in the management of your data
- speedier execution
- compact programs

Then, too, there's that delicious sense of satisfaction when you can say: "No, it's not in BASIC. I wrote it in assembly language."

The programs we will write in assembly language are much different than programs written in BASIC. Each line of a BASIC program is translated by another program (called a BASIC interpreter) into several lines of assembly level code. An example will serve to illustrate this one-to-many translation. Suppose we write an algebraic statement in BASIC: $Z = X + Y$. Let's see the assembly level statements that could be used to accomplish this.

1. Go get the value of X and place it in the accumulator. (The accumulator is the spot where the addition will take place.)
2. Set up a pointer to the location where the value of Y is stored.
3. Add the accumulator contents to the value the pointer locates. (The sum will be left in the accumulator.)
4. Store the contents of the accumulator in the location belonging to Z.

The assembly level statements are the closest to the actual computer actions that a programmer may specify. Each statement written in assembly language is translated by another program (called an assembler) into one machine instruction.

All machine instructions are strings of Øs and 1s. One example is

10111000

Now this may make perfect sense to a computer, but humans tend to think better in words. This is where assembly language comes in. It allows the programmer to refer to the instructions in word-like abbreviations called mnemonics.

In this text we will be studying most of the instructions available to the programmer of the Z-8Ø microprocessor. In each case we will learn

1. how the instruction works
2. the mnemonic
3. the machine code (OP code)

The job of the assembly language programmer is to know how the instructions can do the job he needs done and to write the instruction mnemonics. The job of the assembler program is to translate the mnemonics into machine code. The job of the computer is to execute the machine code instructions. Two other programs may be involved in this process. A text editor program is usually used to write the mnemonics into a text file, usually maintained on a tape or disk system. A load program (or loader) is used to input the machine code (often called an object file) into the computer's memory for execution. The whole process can be summarized as follows.

Programmer designs program and writes mnemonics.

Programmer keys mnemonics in using text editor program. He creates a text file in computer memory or on tape or disk.

Assembler program translates mnemonics into machine code and creates an object file in computer memory or on tape or disk.

Loader program brings object file into computer for execution.

Programmer runs program for testing and debugging.

The emphasis in this text is on the steps of design and coding. Running the text editor, assembler, and loader is just a matter of following the specific instructions included with the particular versions running on your system. Some specific help on how to debug your programs can be found in the final chapter of this book.

1

bits, bytes, and boolean operators

Binary and Hexadecimal Number Systems

The binary number system is the basis of computer operations. It requires the use of only two digits: Ø and 1. These two possibilities can be easily represented by a low and high voltage, respectively. The decimal numbers Ø through 5 appear below written in binary form.

$$
\begin{aligned}
Ø &= Ø \\
1 &= 1 \\
1Ø &= 2 \\
11 &= 3 \\
1ØØ &= 4 \\
1Ø1 &= 5
\end{aligned}
$$

It can be seen that the numbers rapidly become very long.

In the decimal system each digit represents a power of 1Ø. For example

$$
\begin{aligned}
423 = \quad &4 \times 1ØØ = \quad 4 \times 1Ø^2 \\
&+ 2 \times 1Ø \quad + 2 \times 1Ø^1 \\
&+ 3 \times 1 \quad\ \ + 3 \times 1Ø^0
\end{aligned}
$$

(Any number raised to the Ø power is 1. So, $2^0 = 1$, $1Ø^0 = 1$, and $16^0 = 1$.)

In the binary system, each digit represents a power of 2.

$$
\begin{aligned}
11Ø1 = \quad &1 \times 2^3 = \quad 1 \times 8 \\
&+ 1 \times 2^2 \quad + 1 \times 4 \\
&+ Ø \times 2^1 \quad + Ø \times 2 \\
&+ 1 \times 2^0 \quad + 1 \times 1
\end{aligned}
$$

So 11Ø1 in binary is the equivalent of 13 in decimal. Conversion between the two number systems can be done using these rules, but it is not common to have to convert numbers larger than 15 back and forth. Larger numbers are generally first converted into the hexadecimal system.

In the hexadecimal, or base 16, number system, there are 16 different digits. The digits Ø-9 are borrowed from the decimal system, and letters of the alphabet fill in for the other six.

$$A = 10$$
$$B = 11$$
$$C = 12$$
$$D = 13$$
$$E = 14$$
$$F = 15$$

In the hexadecimal system, each digit represents a power of 16.

$$1B3 = \quad 1 \times 16^2 = \quad 1 \times 256$$
$$+ \; B \times 16^1 \quad + \; 11 \times 16$$
$$+ \; 3 \times 16^0 \quad + \; 3 \times 1$$

So 1B3 (hexadecimal) is the equivalent of 435 in the decimal system.

With three number systems in use, some way to distinguish between them is necessary. Whenever confusion could arise, we will use a subscripted letter to distinguish between the systems.

$$10_H — \text{Hexadecimal}$$
$$10_D — \text{Decimal}$$
$$10_B — \text{Binary}$$

Converting Between the Systems

Conversions of small numbers can be done using the following chart.

Decimal	Binary	Hexadecimal
0	0	0
1	1	1
2	10	2
3	11	3
4	100	4
5	101	5
6	110	6
7	111	7
8	1000	8
9	1001	9
10	1010	A
11	1011	B
12	1100	C
13	1101	D
14	1110	E
15	1111	F
16	10000	10

Hexadecimal–Decimal

Hexadecimal numbers can be converted into the decimal system most easily by using the powers of 16. The following example shows how to convert $2AF3_H$ to decimal.

$$
\begin{array}{llll}
2 \times 16^3 = & 2 \times 4096 = & 8192 = & 10{,}995_D \\
+ \; A \times 16^2 & + \; 10 \times 256 & + \; 2560 & \\
+ \; F \times 16^1 & + \; 15 \times 16 & + \; 240 & \\
+ \; 3 \times 16^0 & + \; 3 \times 1 & + \; 3 &
\end{array}
$$

Conversions from decimal to hexadecimal can be done using division and the following chart of powers of 16.

Powers of 16

16^0 = 1
16^1 = 16
16^2 = 256
16^3 = 4,096
16^4 = 65,536

Numbers larger than 16^4 are rarely encountered. We will always begin by dividing by the largest power of 16 that will fit. Beginning with $10{,}995_D$, here's how to get back to $2AF3_H$.

$$
\begin{array}{r}
2 \; r \; 2803 \\
4096 \overline{\smash{\big)} 10{,}995}
\end{array}
\qquad\qquad 2
$$

$$
\begin{array}{r}
10 \; r \; 243 \\
256 \overline{\smash{\big)} 2803}
\end{array}
\qquad\qquad A
$$

$$
\begin{array}{r}
15 \; r \; 3 \\
16 \overline{\smash{\big)} 243}
\end{array}
\qquad\qquad F
$$

$$
\begin{array}{r}
3 \\
1 \overline{\smash{\big)} 3}
\end{array}
\qquad\qquad 3
$$

Hexadecimal–Binary

Conversions between hexadecimal and binary are extremely easy. Every hexadecimal digit can be translated into four binary digits using the conversion chart. For example,

$$53D_H = 101 \quad 0011 \quad 1101_B$$

Binary numbers can be converted to hexadecimal by counting off groups of four digits beginning from the right. Then each group is translated into a hexadecimal digit. Thus,

$$1011101101_B = 10 \quad 1110 \quad 1101_B \quad = 2ED_H$$

Bits and Bytes

A bit is the unit of storage required to hold one binary digit. We will denote a bit by enclosing the 0 or 1 value in a box as shown.

$$\boxed{0} \text{ or } \boxed{1}$$

Sometimes bits are important in themselves, but usually they are considered in groups. A group of eight bits is called a byte. We will denote a byte as a string of eight boxes.

$$\boxed{1}\boxed{0}\boxed{1}\boxed{0}\boxed{0}\boxed{1}\boxed{0}\boxed{1}$$

Since four bits make one hexadecimal digit, it takes two hexadecimal digits to describe the contents of a byte. Sometimes a group of four bits is called a nibble.

The byte is the basic arithmetic unit of a microcomputer. If we only want to count, the highest number we can count to in a byte is 255.

$$\boxed{1}\boxed{1}\boxed{1}\boxed{1}\boxed{1}\boxed{1}\boxed{1}\boxed{1} = FF_H = 255_D$$

We also have the capability of adding two positive numbers, so long as they do not total more than 255. But how can we subtract? Subtraction requires the ability to express negative numbers.

2's Complement Representation

We would like to have the ability to represent negative as well as positive numbers. This is accomplished by reserving one of the eight bits as an indicator of the sign of the number.

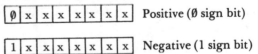

$$\boxed{0}\boxed{x}\boxed{x}\boxed{x}\boxed{x}\boxed{x}\boxed{x}\boxed{x} \text{ Positive (0 sign bit)}$$

$$\boxed{1}\boxed{x}\boxed{x}\boxed{x}\boxed{x}\boxed{x}\boxed{x}\boxed{x} \text{ Negative (1 sign bit)}$$

By tying up one of the eight bits to indicate the sign, we are left with only seven bits for the magnitude of the number. So the highest number we can count to is 127.

$$\boxed{0}\boxed{1}\boxed{1}\boxed{1}\boxed{1}\boxed{1}\boxed{1}\boxed{1} = 7F_H = 127_D$$

So how would we represent -127? A first try might be to simply reverse the sign bit and leave all the magnitude bits unchanged. Although this scheme is easy to understand, it turns out to be very difficult to work with.

A second try might be to reverse all the bits. This is called 1's complement.

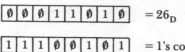

If we used this method to represent negative numbers, let's see where it would lead. We would certainly want 26 and − 26 to add up to zero. But

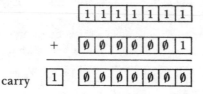

when we'd really like all Øs. However, if we add 1 and ignore the carry, we get just what we want:

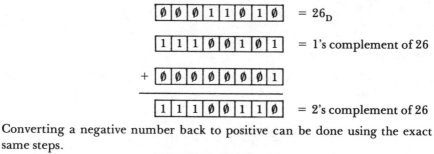

Out of this reasoning came 2's complement representation of negative numbers. 2's complement is formed by adding 1 to the 1's complement form.

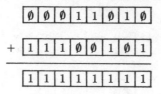

Converting a negative number back to positive can be done using the exact same steps.

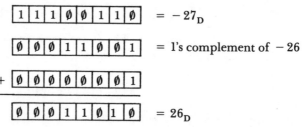

Byte-Size Arithmetic

We are now equipped to perform addition and subtraction of binary numbers. Here are some examples.

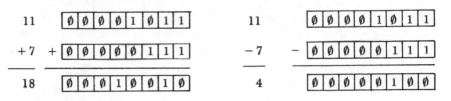

11	Ø Ø Ø Ø 1 Ø 1 1		11	Ø Ø Ø Ø 1 Ø 1 1
+ 7	+ Ø Ø Ø Ø Ø 1 1 1		− 7	− Ø Ø Ø Ø Ø 1 1 1
18	Ø Ø Ø 1 Ø Ø 1 Ø		4	Ø Ø Ø Ø Ø 1 Ø Ø

Arithmetic Flags

We have already seen one of the arithmetic flags, the carry flag. It is set whenever the result of an addition is larger than eight bits.

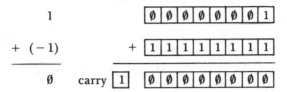

1	Ø Ø Ø Ø Ø Ø Ø 1
+ (− 1)	+ 1 1 1 1 1 1 1 1
Ø carry 1	Ø Ø Ø Ø Ø Ø Ø Ø

In addition the carry bit is most often just ignored. It is simply a by-product of 2's complement representation.

In subtraction the carry bit has more meaning.

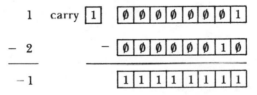

1 carry 1	Ø Ø Ø Ø Ø Ø Ø 1
− 2	− Ø Ø Ø Ø Ø Ø 1 Ø
−1	1 1 1 1 1 1 1 1

Here it is when a borrow is generated. Thus the carry bit tells us that we subtracted a number from a smaller number.

The overflow flag is an indication that something's gone wrong. We know that an eight bit number with one sign bit and seven magnitude bits cannot be larger than 127. The smallest it can be is − 128.

$$\boxed{1\ \text{Ø}\ \text{Ø}\ \text{Ø}\ \text{Ø}\ \text{Ø}\ \text{Ø}\ \text{Ø}} \quad = -128_D$$

Now suppose we try to add 75 and 80:

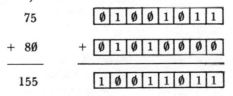

75	Ø 1 Ø Ø 1 Ø 1 1
+ 8Ø	+ Ø 1 Ø 1 Ø Ø Ø Ø
155	1 Ø Ø 1 1 Ø 1 1

What has happened is that the magnitude bits have carried over into the sign bit, making the result look like a negative number. The overflow flag is then set to indicate that the answer is unreliable. This can also happen when two large negative numbers are added. The overflow flag is again set to point up the trouble.

(− 75)		1 Ø 1 1 Ø 1 Ø 1
+ (− 8Ø)	+	1 Ø 1 1 Ø Ø Ø Ø
− 155	1	Ø 1 1 Ø Ø 1 Ø 1

Again the sign bit was reversed. The carry flag was also set, but that is unimportant.

If the two operands to be added are of opposite sign, no overflow can occur.

Two other flags are very simple in their operation. The sign flag indicates whether the result of an arithmetic operation is positive or negative. It is an exact copy of the sign bit, so Ø means the result was positive and 1 indicates a negative result. Since a zero result has a Ø sign bit, it is obviously considered to be a positive number. A zero result, however, is so important that it is reported in a flag all its own. The zero flag is set when the result is zero.

Summary of Eight Bit Arithmetic Flags

Carry (C)	—	Carry out of the eight bits 1: occurred Ø: did not occur
Overflow (V)	—	Sign bit clobbered 1: occurred Ø: did not occur
Sign (S)	—	Result was 1: negative Ø: positive
Zero (Z)	—	Zero result 1: occurred Ø: did not occur

Boolean Operators

Arithmetic is not the only thing that can be done to pairs of eight bit values. There is the whole class of logical, or Boolean, operators. Boolean operators treat all eight bits alike, with no sign bit.

AND

The AND operator compares two bytes bit by bit. If a bit is set in both operands, it is set to 1 in the result. Otherwise the bit is reset to Ø in the result. This operation is summarized in the following table.

A	B	A AND B
1	1	1
1	Ø	Ø
Ø	1	Ø
Ø	Ø	Ø

Using this table, each of the bits in a byte is set or reset in turn, as in the following example.

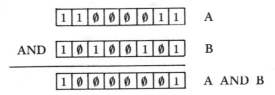

OR

The OR operator compares two bytes bit by bit. If a bit is set in either operand, it is set in the result. Otherwise it is reset in the result.

A	B	A OR B
1	1	1
1	Ø	1
Ø	1	1
Ø	Ø	Ø

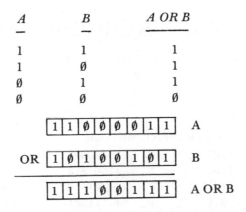

XOR

The XOR (exclusive OR) operator compares the two bytes bit by bit. If the bit is set in either operand, but *not* in both, it is set in the result. Otherwise it is reset in the result.

A	B	A XOR B
1	1	Ø
1	Ø	1
Ø	1	1
Ø	Ø	Ø

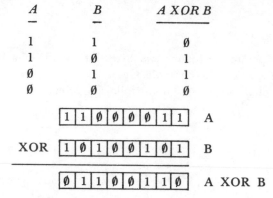

Flags and the Binary Operators

Carry   —   Reset by AND, OR, and XOR

Zero   —   Indicates that all bits of the result are zero
         1: occurred
         Ø: did not occur

Sign   —   Set to the value in the uppermost bit (same as arithmetic operation)

Logical operations affect the parity flag instead of the overflow flag. The parity flag tells whether an even or an odd number of bits are set in the result. The parity flag is set when an even number of bits are set in the result. The flag is reset when an odd number of bits are set in the result.

Result | 1 | Ø | 1 | 1 | 1 | Ø | 1 | Ø | (five bits set)
           P = Ø

Result | 1 | Ø | Ø | Ø | Ø | Ø | Ø | 1 | (two bits set)
           P = 1

Exercises

1. Convert the following numbers to decimal.

a.	1Ø1	e.	1ØØØØØØØ	i.	ØØØ1ØØ1Ø
b.	11Ø1	f.	11ØØ1Ø1Ø	j.	Ø111ØØ11
c.	111Ø1	g.	1ØØØ111Ø	k.	111ØØØ1ØØ
d.	1Ø1Ø11	h.	11111ØØ1	l.	1Ø1Ø1Ø1Ø11

2. Convert the following decimal numbers to hexadecimal and then from hexadecimal to binary.

a.	6	e.	542	i.	15,430
b.	14	f.	1077	j.	43,751
c.	127	g.	4095	k.	65,552
d.	280	h.	8702	l.	70,980

3. Give the eight-bit signed representation of the following positive numbers. Then convert each to 2's complement.

a.	7	c.	23	e.	104
b.	17	d.	48	f.	127

4. Given the following bytes with one sign bit and seven magnitude bits, give the decimal equivalent of their contents.

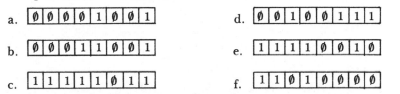

a. 0 0 0 0 1 0 0 1   d. 0 0 1 0 0 1 1 1

b. 0 0 0 1 1 0 0 1   e. 1 1 1 1 0 0 1 0

c. 1 1 1 1 1 0 1 1   f. 1 1 0 1 0 0 0 0

5. Perform the following arithmetic operations in binary form. For each, give the result in binary, and tell whether the carry and/or overflow flags are set.

a. 11 + 15
b. 17 + (− 21)
c. 46 − 12
d. 104 + 55
e. (− 67) − 107
f. (− 67) + 107

6. For each of the following pairs of bytes, find their AND, OR, and XOR. Indicate what flags are set.

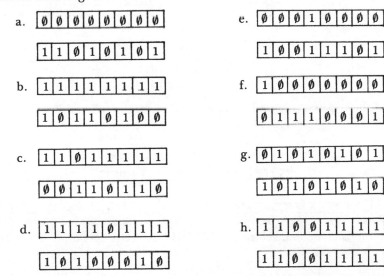

a. 0 0 0 0 0 0 0 0
   1 1 0 1 0 1 0 1

b. 1 1 1 1 1 1 1 1
   1 0 1 1 0 1 0 0

c. 1 1 0 1 1 1 1 1
   0 0 1 1 0 1 1 0

d. 1 1 1 1 0 1 1 1
   1 0 1 0 0 0 1 0

e. 0 0 0 1 0 0 0 0
   1 0 0 1 1 1 0 1

f. 1 0 0 0 0 0 0 0
   0 1 1 1 0 0 0 1

g. 0 1 0 1 0 1 0 1
   1 0 1 0 1 0 1 0

h. 1 1 0 0 1 1 1 1
   1 1 0 0 1 1 1 1

2

where is my variable?

The Higher Level Language Programmer

Whatever else the higher level language programmer may know about his program, he probably has very little sense of where his variables are located. Consider the following program:

$$X = 3$$
$$Y = 2$$
$$Z = X + Y$$
$$\text{PRINT } Z$$

Where is X? Where is Y? Where does the addition take place? The whole "where" aspect is generally quite foreign to the new assembly language programmer. Also missing is the language needed to talk about "where" topics.

Registers

The registers are one of the most common answers to a "where" question. Here is a diagram of the 8080 register set. (The Z-80 has these and more.)

A	Flags
B	C
D	E
H	L

Each of the registers is eight bits long. The bits are numbered from right to left. All of the registers look alike. Here is a close-up of one of the registers.

Bit # 7 6 5 4 3 2 1 0

| 1 | 0 | 1 | 0 | 1 | 0 | 1 | 0 | Register E

The A register is the answer to the question: "Where does the addition take place?" Also called the accumulator, register A always holds one of the two operands in an add, subtract, AND, OR, or XOR operation. The result

14

is also left in register A. So every arithmetic and logical operation is of the form

$$X \leftarrow X \triangle Y$$

The register labeled "Flags" is where the carry, overflow, and other flag bits are stored. It is usually accessed only one bit at a time.

Registers B and C, D and E, and H and L may be treated as register pairs. Then the two eight bit registers may instead be regarded as one 16 bit register. Besides being able to house a larger number, the main use of 16 bit values in a microcomputer is to address memory.

Memory

Memory is the most likely answer to the question concerning the whereabouts of any variable. It also answers the question "Where is my program?"

Memory is divided into individual bytes. Each byte in memory has a unique address. Addresses in the 8080 and Z-80 are all two bytes in length. How much memory can be addressed in two bytes? Consider the following progression.

# of Bits	Size of Memory	Highest Address in Hexadecimal
8	256 bytes (0–255)	FF
9	512 bytes	1FF
10	1024 bytes = 1k	3FF
11	2048 bytes = 2k	7FF
12	4096 bytes = 4k	FFF
13	8192 bytes = 8k	1FFF
14	16,384 bytes = 16k	3FFF
15	32,768 bytes = 32k	7FFF
16	65,536 bytes = 64k	FFFF

One byte addresses only allow for ¼k of memory. Since this is usually inadequate, the logical choice was to go to two bytes for an address. A two byte address allows the possibility of addressing 64k of memory.

We have already mentioned that the BC, DE, and HL register pairs may be used to contain memory addresses. There are, in addition, two other 16 bit memory address registers common to the 8080 and Z-80 microprocessors.

Stack Pointer and Program Counter

The stack pointer (SP) is a 16 bit register whose only function is to point to a location in memory.

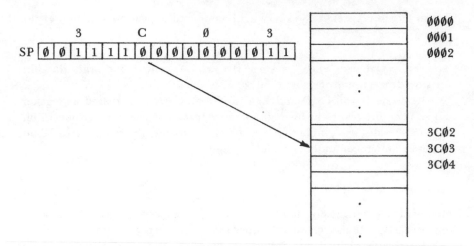

In the Z-80 microprocessor, the stack is just a designated portion of regular memory. The programmer sets the stack to the location of his choosing. With the question "Where is the stack?" out of the way, a good question to consider next is "What is the stack?"

A stack, in the general sense, is a collection of items where all additions and all deletions occur at the top. A stack of dishes, for example, fits this description.

      The stack   Addition to   Deletion from
                     the stack   the stack

The characteristic of a stack is that only the top is accessible.

The stack in the Z-80 or 8080 sense is a region of memory where values can be saved temporarily. Its most common use comes in relation to subroutine calls, but it can be used to store intermediate results in a computation, or any short-lived variable. Use of the stack for these purposes saves having to use a separate, unique memory location for transient data.

The program counter is also a 16 bit register which points to an address in memory. That address is located within the program that is currently running, and contains the next instruction to be executed.

Notation

Suppose we have a variable located in memory which we have called VAR-BLE. Since VARBLE is located in memory, it has an address. It also has a value. So when we use VARBLE, which do we mean, the address or the value? To the higher level language programmer there can be no problem. He knows nothing of the whereabouts of his variables. When he uses VARBLE he means its value.

The assembly language programmer will deal with both values and addresses. It is the instructions themselves which will clarify the usage. Some instructions operate on values, others deal with addresses. But to talk about the instructions requires a new notation. In this context, n will denote an eight bit number, and nn a 16 bit number. So we will use

> nn as the address, and
> (nn) as the value

Mnemonics

To the microprocessor, an instruction is a bit pattern called an OP code. The binary values are most often written in hexadecimal. To the human, a bunch of numbers, hexadecimal or binary, are difficult to relate to. Mnemonics are short, word-like abbreviations for the instructions which are translated into their numeric equivalents by a program called an assembler.

For each of the instructions we will be studying the hexadecimal OP code and mnemonic will be given. Mnemonics for the 8080 and Z-80 are not the same even though the OP code and instruction execution are. So both mnemonics will be given. In addition, note that the TDL Z-80 assembler uses 8080 mnemonics.

Eight Bit Load Instructions

Register–Register

The contents of any eight bit register can be moved to any other eight bit register.

> MOV   E,A   (8080)
> LD   E,A   (Z-80)

The contents of register A would then be moved into register E (to E from A). The target is listed first. This class of load instructions is denoted

> MOV   r,r '   (8080)
> LD   r,r '   (Z-80)

where r and r' can be any of A, B, C, D, E, H, and L, and the action is r ◄─ r'.

The OP code for our sample instruction (E ◄─ A) is $5F_H$. Here is a chart which gives the OP codes for all register-register moves.

		Source Register						
		A	B	C	D	E	H	L
	A	7F	78	79	7A	7B	7C	7D
	B	47	40	41	42	43	44	45
Destination	C	4F	48	49	4A	4B	4C	4D
Register	D	57	50	51	52	53	54	55
	E	5F	58	59	5A	5B	5C	5D
	H	67	60	61	62	63	64	65
	L	6F	68	69	6A	6B	6C	6D

Register-Memory

Eight bit values can be loaded from memory into the registers and from the registers to memory. Movements between the accumulator (register A) and memory can be accomplished in several different ways. Movements between memory and any other register are very restricted.

We mentioned that the register pairs BC, DE, and HL can be used as pointers to memory. The HL pair is by far the most commonly used for this purpose. Suppose we have the following situation.

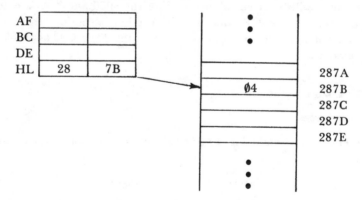

The HL register points to memory location 287B which contains the value 04_H. This value can be loaded into any of the eight bit registers using the instruction

```
MOV      r,m      (8080)
LD       r,(HL)   (Z-80)
```

In the 8Ø8Ø mnemonic, M indicates a memory reference and always refers to the memory location pointed to by the HL pair.

In this instruction, the movement can be depicted as

$$r \leftarrow (HL)$$

Movement in the opposite direction is also possible:

$$(HL) \leftarrow r$$

Here the contents of any eight bit register can be stored in the memory location pointed to by the HL pair. The instructions are

MOV	M,r	(8Ø8Ø)
LD	(HL),r	(Z-8Ø)

Both of these instructions have separate OP codes for each eight bit register. The OP codes are summarized in the following table.

	A	B	C	D	E	H	L
r ← (HL)	7E	46	4E	56	5E	66	6E
(HL) ← r	77	7Ø	71	72	73	74	75

Register A–Memory

Additional movements between the accumulator and memory are possible. Four of them are just like the register-memory (HL) instructions just described. They are summarized in the following table.

Action	OP Code	8Ø8Ø Mnemonic		Z-8Ø Mnemonic	
A←(BC)	ØA	LDAX	B	LD	A, (BC)
A←(DE)	1A	LDAX	D	LD	A, (DE)
(BC)←A	Ø2	STAX	B	LD	(BC), A
(DE)←A	12	STAX	D	LD	(DE), A

Missing so far in all these register-memory movements is the ability to load the value of a variable by name. That is,

$$A \leftarrow (VARBLE)$$

or

$$(VARBLE) \leftarrow A$$

Both of these actions are possible, but more information than just the OP code is required. Besides telling the computer we want to load a variable from memory, we have to tell it which one.

Before, when we wanted to load a location from memory, we answered the question "Which one?" with "The one pointed to by the HL (or BC, or DE) pair." So the location didn't have to be contained in the instruction. This time we will have to give the location.

LDA   VARBLE   (8080)
LD   A, (VARBLE)   (Z-80)

We give the assembler the name of the variable. The assembler translates the name into its two byte address. (It keeps a symbol table for this purpose.)

Suppose VARBLE is stored at location 23F3. Then this address would become part of the instruction. One byte would be used for the OP code and two for the address, so the whole instruction would be three bytes long. Here are the possibilities (nn stands for the variable name in the mnemonic and for its address in the instruction).

Operation	OP Code	8080 Mnemonic	Z-80 Mnemonic
A←(nn)	3Ann	LDA nn	LD A,(nn)
(nn)←A	32nn	STA nn	LD (nn), A

Register–Immediate

Suppose we want to place a certain value into a register or memory location.

$$A \leftarrow 7$$

The number 7 is an absolute value, or an immediate. We can store any eight bit absolute value into any of the eight bit registers or into the memory location pointed to by the HL register pair.

The absolute value desired is written with the mnemonic and is assembled directly into the instruction. The instruction then becomes two bytes long.

MVI   C, − 27   (8080)
LD   C, − 27   (Z-80)

After executing this instruction, register C would then contain

C [1|1|1|0|0|1|0|1]   (− 27 in 2's complement form)

The possibilities are charted below. The letter n stands for the eight bit absolute value.

Operation	8080 Mnemonic	Z-80 Mnemonic
r←n	MVI r,n	LD r,n
(HL)←n	MVI M,n	LD (HL),n

The OP codes for the immediate instructions are presented in the following table.

	A	B	C	D	E	H	L	(HL)
s ← n	3En	Ø6n	ØEn	16n	1En	26n	2En	36n

Here s stands for r or (HL) and n is in 2's complement form if negative.

Z-80 Indexed Eight Bit load and Store

Two other 16 bit registers exist in the Z-80 microprocessor. These are the IX and IY index registers.

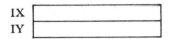

Like the stack pointer and program counter, these registers are used exclusively to point to memory locations. Like the HL pair, they are generally used to point to variables in memory.

The index registers can, however, be used with a displacement. A displacement is an eight bit signed number which is coded directly into the instruction. Here is an illustration of how the index registers work.

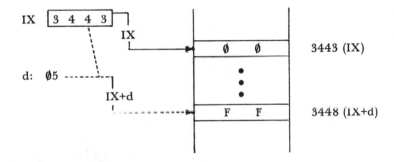

In this illustration the IX index register points to memory location 3443_H. The value of the displacement is 05_H. So the location that would be affected by the instruction would be $3443_{11} + 05_H = 3448_H$. Take for example the following load instruction into the B register.

```
MOV     B,5(X)      (TDL Z-80)
LD      B, (IX + 5)  (Z-80)
```

At the conclusion of the operation register B would contain FF_H, not 00.

The displacement is a signed eight bit number. So its values can range from -128 to $+127$.

Indexed instructions can be tricky to deal with, and much will be said later about techniques for using them.

Diagramatically, the load and store index instructions fall into one of three categories. Here ii will mean the IX or IY index register. Note that an immediate can be loaded into an indexed memory location.

$$r \leftarrow (ii + d)$$
$$(ii + d) \leftarrow r$$
$$(ii + d) \leftarrow n$$

Since the displacement is coded into the instruction, the instruction must be at least two bytes long. In fact, it is three bytes long. Two bytes are used for the OP code. Most of the Z-80 instructions which are extensions of the 8080 instruction set are two bytes long. All of the IX index OP codes begin with DD and the IY with FD. Index instructions which include an immediate are four bytes long.

Here, then, are the OP codes for the Z-80 index instructions.

	A	B	C	D	E	H	L
r ← (IX+d)	DD7Ed	DD46d	DD4Ed	DD56d	DD5Ed	DD66d	DD6Ed
r ← (IY+d)	FD7Ed	FD46d	FD4Ed	FD56d	FD5Ed	FD66d	FD6Ed
(IX+d) ← r	DD77d	DD70d	DD71d	DD72d	DD73d	DD74d	DD75d
(IY+d) ← r	FD77d	FD70d	FD71d	FD72d	FD73d	FD74d	FD75d

(IX+d) ← n   DD36dn

(IY+d) ← n   FD36dn

16 Bit Load and Store Instructions

Register Summary

Before going further, let's take a moment to review the registers discussed so far:

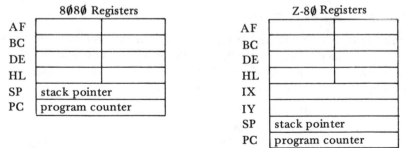

Register-Register

We saw that it was possible to move the contents of any eight bit register to any other eight bit register. Movements between 16 bit registers are, by contrast, almost nonexistent. Only the stack pointer (SP) can receive a value from another 16 bit register. Even then, there are only three possibilities.

Action	OP Code	TDL Z-80 & 8080 Mnemonic	Z-80 Mnemonic
SP←HL	F9	SPHL	LD SP,HL
SP←IX*	DDF9	SPIX	LD SP,IX
SP←IY*	FDF9	SPIY	LD SP,IY

*Z-80 only.

Memory-Register

In the eight bit load instructions it was possible to load and store values from memory locations pointed to by the HL pair, r←(HL). This does not occur for 16 bit registers at all. We also saw that the contents of a one byte variable could be loaded into the accumulator by referencing its name. A two byte variable can be loaded or stored in the HL pair by referencing its name.

$$\text{LHLD} \quad \text{BIGVAR} \qquad (8080)$$
$$\text{LD} \qquad \text{HL, (BIGVAR)} \quad (\text{Z-80})$$

Here, the contents of the address BIGVAR and the address BIGVAR + 1 are loaded into the HL pair.

   Swapped Format. A two byte variable is stored in memory in what is known as swapped format. By this is meant that the low order byte is loaded at the lower memory address. An example should make this clear. Suppose BIGVAR is stored at location 1F23.

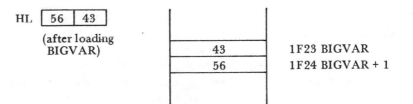

HL │ 56 │ 43 │
(after loading BIGVAR)

| 43 | 1F23 BIGVAR |
| 56 | 1F24 BIGVAR + 1 |

Two byte variables are not the only numbers stored in swapped format. If an 8080 or Z-80 instruction contains within it a two byte address, that address is stored in swapped format. Our example load instruction has OP code 2A and the address of BIGVAR is contained within the instruction, so the instruction in hexadecimal would be

$$2A\ 231F$$

This ability to load and store a named 16 bit variable exists in 8080 for the HL register pair only. The Z-80 microprocessor possesses this capability for the

BC, DE, HL, SP, IX, and IY registers. Here are the instructions and OP codes (nn stands for the two byte address, and rr for the register name).

	Operation	OP Code	TDL Z-80 and 8080 Mnemonic	Z-80 Mnemonic
8080	HL ←(nn)	2Ann	LHLD nn	LD HL,(nn)
&	(nn)←HL	22nn	SHLD nn	LD (nn),HL
Z-80				
Z-80	BC ←(nn)	ED4Bnn	LBCD nn	LD BC,(nn)
only	(nn)← BC	ED43nn	SBCD nn	LD (nn),BC
	DE ←(nn)	ED5Bnn	LDED nn	LD DE,(nn)
	(nn)← DE	ED53nn	SDED nn	LD (nn),DE
	SP ←(nn)	ED7Bnn	LSPD nn	LD SP,(nn)
	(nn)← SP	ED73nn	SSPD nn	LD (nn),SP
	IX ←(nn)	DD2Ann	LIXD nn	LD IX,(nn)
	(nn)← IX	DD22nn	SIXD nn	LD (nn),IX
	IY ←(nn)	FD2Ann	LIYD nn	LD IY,(nn)
	(nn)← IY	FD22nn	SIYD nn	LD (nn),IY

Register–Immediate

Just as a one byte immediate could be loaded into any eight bit register, so can a two byte immediate be loaded into any 16 bit (double eight bit) register. Usually that value is an address.

$$\begin{array}{lll} \text{LXI} & \text{H,BIGVAR} & \text{(8080)} \\ \text{LD} & \text{HL,BIGVBAR} & \text{(Z-80)} \end{array}$$

The above instruction has the effect of loading BIGVAR'S address (not its value) into the HL pair. Diagrammatically,

$$rr \leftarrow nn$$

A constant can also be loaded using these same instructions.

The 8080 possesses all of these immediate instructions except the two that reference the IX and IY index registers. The OP codes are given below.

	BC	DE	HL	SP	IX	IY
rr ← nn	01nn	11nn	21nn	31nn	DD21nn	FD21nn

The mnemonics for these are

$$\begin{array}{lll} \text{LXI} & \text{rr,nn} & \text{(8080)} \\ \text{LD} & \text{rr,nn} & \text{(Z-80)} \end{array}$$

Note that the meaning of rr differs for the 8080 and Z-80. The Z-80 uses any one of BC, DE, HL, SP, IX, or IY. The 8080 uses B for BC, D for DE, H for HL, and SP for SP. The TDL assembler uses the 8080 form and, in addition, X for IX and Y for IY.

PUSH and POP Instructions

PUSH and POP instructions transfer values back and forth between register pairs and the stack. For this purpose the A register and the flag register are treated as a pair.

In a PUSH instruction, the contents of a registered pair are stored on the stack, and the stack pointer is adjusted. The stack always grows from high to low addresses, so to add an item to the stack the stack pointer must be decremented.

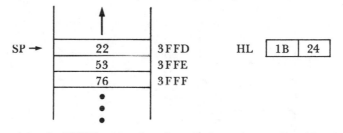

The execution of a PUSH action has four distinct phases. Consider the action of pushing the contents of the HL pair onto the stack:

1. The stack pointer is decremented.

2. The high order byte (register H) is stored.

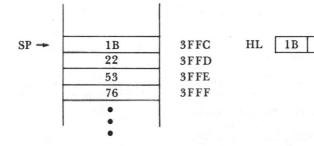

3. The stack pointer is decremented again.

```
SP →  ┌──────────┐
      │          │  3FFB        HL  ┌─────┬─────┐
      ├──────────┤                  │ 1B  │ 24  │
      │    1B    │  3FFC            └─────┴─────┘
      ├──────────┤
      │    22    │  3FFD
      ├──────────┤
      │    53    │  3FFE
      ├──────────┤
      │    76    │  3FFF
      │     •    │
      │     •    │
      │     •    │
      └──────────┘
```

4. The low order byte (register L) is stored.

```
SP →  ┌──────────┐
      │    24    │  3FFB
      ├──────────┤
      │    1B    │  3FFC
      ├──────────┤
      │    22    │  3FFD
      ├──────────┤
      │    53    │  3FFE
      ├──────────┤
      │    76    │  3FFF
      │     •    │
      │     •    │
      │     •    │
      └──────────┘
```

The POP instruction is the exact opposite of PUSH. For both the 8080 and Z-80 the mnemonics are the same:

PUSH   rr
POP   rr

Again rr is expressed differently for the two mnemonic versions, as was previously discussed. Also, the A–Flag register pair is referred to as PSW (which stands for program status word) in 8080 mnemonics and AF in Z-80 mnemonics. Note that the stack pointer itself cannot be pushed or popped. The relevant OP codes are

	8080 & Z-80				Z-80 only	
	AF	BC	DE	HL	IX	IY
PUSH	F5	C5	D5	E5	DDE5	FDE5
POP	F1	C1	D1	E1	DDE1	FDE1

Exchange Instructions

Exchange instructions swap register contents, or contents of sets of registers. The 8080 instruction set includes only two such instructions. The Z-80 has six. The two common to both perform the following actions.

$$HL \longleftrightarrow DE$$
$$HH \longleftrightarrow (SP)$$

So the contents of the HL register can be exchanged with the contents of the DE register or with the contents of the top of the stack.

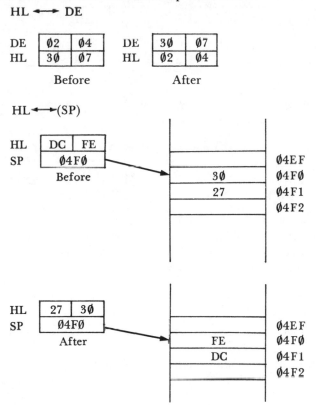

Mnemonics and OP codes for these are

Exchange	OP Code	8080 Mnemonic	Z-80 Mnemonic
HL ⟷ DE	EB	XCHG	EX DE,HL
HL ⟷ (SP)	E3	XTHL	EX (SP),HL

The Z-80 has the capability to exchange either the IX or IY index register with the top of the stack as well.

Action	OP Code	TDL Z-80 Mnemonic	Z-80 Mnemonic
(SP) ⟷ IX	DDE3	XTIX	EX (SP),IX
(SP) ⟷ IY	FDE3	XTIY	EX (SP),IY

The two other Z-8Ø exchange instructions swap sets of registers. Besides all the Z-8Ø registers given so far, the Z-8Ø has a duplicate set of the A and flag registers, and of registers BC, DE, and HL. Exchange instructions swap either AF and AF′ or BC, DE, HL and BC′, DE′, HL′. The swaps appear as

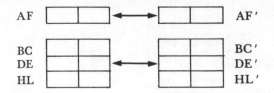

The prime set cannot be addressed or acted on in any way except to swap with the current set, which then becomes dormant.

Action	OP Code	TDL Z-8Ø Mnemonic	Z-8Ø Mnemonic
AF ◄──►AF′	Ø8	EXAF	EX AF,AF′
BCDEHL ◄──►BCDEHL′	D9	EXX	EXX

The main purpose for these exchange instructions is to provide a very fast way of saving contents of all the registers. It is important to note that the only way to access the saved register is to swap back. No values may be exchanged directly between the two sets of registers.

Exercises

1. Write a sequence of instructions that will swap the contents of the D and E registers.

2. What will the B register contain after execution of this instruction? (The − 12 is decimal.)

```
MVI     B, − 12     (8Ø8Ø)
LD      B, − 12     (Z-8Ø)
```

3. Suppose the HL pair and the given memory locations contain the values illustrated below.

HL | 2Ø | 3D |

•	
•	
ØØ	2Ø39
42	2Ø3A
ØØ	2Ø3B
F3	2Ø3C
39	2Ø3D
27	2Ø3E

What will register A contain after the following sequence of instructions?

8080	Z-80
MOV L,M	LD L, (HL)
MOV A,M	LD A, (IIL)

4. Using swapped format, give the hexadecimal instruction that loads the value of MYVAR (address = 34F3) into the A register.

5. Give the effect of

MOV	E,12(X)	(TDL Z-80)
LD	E,(IX + 12)	(Z-80)

6. Explain the difference between the following pair of instructions.

8080	Z-80
LHLD SPOT	LD HL(SPOT)
LXI H,SPOT	LD HL,SPOT

7. Given the initial register contents

$$AF: 0402_H$$
$$BC: 4020_H$$

what will these registers contain after the following sequence of instructions?

8080	Z-80
PUSH PSW	PUSH AF
PUSH B	PUSH BC
POP PSW	POP AF
POP B	POP BC

8. Would you expect to get the same number back if you tried this sequence of instructions?

8080	Z-80
PUSH H	PUSH HL
SPHL	LD SP,HL
POP H	POP HL

9. Given the memory locations

•	
•	
02	6F32
03	6F33
04	6F34
05	6F35
•	
•	

a. What instruction will set the stack to 6F32?

b. What will register pair BC and the stack pointer contain after execution of
   the following instruction?

POP B	(8080)
POP BC	(Z-80)

10. What does the Z-80 register C contain after execution of the following se-
    quence of instructions?

TDL Z-80	Z-80
MVI A,3	LD A, 3
STA SPOT	LD (SPOT), A
LIXD SPOT	LD IX, (SPOT)
MOV C, − 5 (X)	LD C, (IX − 5)

	21	23 FE
	22	23 FF
SPOT	23	2400
	24	2401
	25	2402
	26	2403
⋮	⋮	⋮

3

a method to our logic

In the first chapter we discussed the form used to store numbers in the microprocessor, the method by which addition and subtraction are performed, and the actions of various logical operators. Now we must discuss the actual instructions which direct these operations. Like the load instructions, we will have two main groups: eight bit and 16 bit instructions.

Eight Bit Arithmetic and Logical Instructions

The accumulator (register A) is the center of activity for most of the eight bit arithmetic and logical instructions. In any two-operand instruction, one of the operands will always be located in the A register. The other operand will always be contained in one of the registers listed below.

8Ø8Ø	Source	Z-8Ø
r	Any eight bit register	r
M	The memory location pointed to by the HL pair	(HL)
n	An immediate (eight bit absolute value)	n
d(X)*	An indexed memory location	(IX + d)
d(Y)*		(IY + d)

*TDL Z-8Ø.

We will refer to any one of these collectively with the letter s.

$$A \leftarrow A + s$$

will describe adding any one of these locations to the accumulator. The 8Ø8Ø version provides a separate mnemonic for use when one of the operands is an immediate.

It will be extremely important to consider the effect on the flags of each of these operations, since the flags provide the programmer with the means of monitoring the run-time execution of his program. The flags pertinent to our work now are

31

C: Set on a carry out of the register.
  Reset otherwise.
Z: Set on a zero result.
  Reset otherwise.
V: Set on overflow into the sign bit.
  Reset otherwise.
S: Set to a copy of the sign bit.
P: Parity flag set if result is even, reset if odd.

Addition

The contents of the accumulator are added to the second operand and the results are left in the accumulator.

Action·	Flags	8080 Mnemonic	Z-80 Mnemonic
A←A + s	C Z V S	ADD s ADI n	ADD A,s

| | 8080 and Z-80 | | | | | | | | | Z-80 only | |
ADD	A	B	C	D	E	H	L	(HL)	n	(IX+d)	(IY+d)
OP code	87	80	81	82	83	84	85	86	C6n	DD86d	FD86d

Addition with Carry

The contents of the accumulator, the second operand, and the carry flag are all added together and the result is left in the accumulator.

Action	Flags	8080 Mnemonic	Z-80 Mnemonic
A←A + s + C	C Z V S	ADC s ACI n	ADC A,s

| | 8080 and Z-80 | | | | | | | | | Z-80 only | |
ADD	A	B	C	D	E	H	L	(HL)	n	(IX+d)	(IY+d)
OP code	8F	88	89	8A	8B	8C	8D	8E	CEn	DD8Ed	FD8Ed

Let's consider for a moment the purpose of an addition with carry. Suppose we are dealing with two very long binary numbers. Each is so long that it takes three bytes to hold the number: 23 magnitude bits and one sign bit.

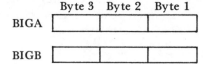

The two numbers can be added using the accumulator and the following game plan.

1. Load byte 1 of BIGA into the accumulator. Add byte 1 of BIGB. Store the result.
2. Load byte 2 of BIGA into the accumulator. Perform an add-with-carry with byte 2 of BIGB. Store the result.
3. Repeat step 2 using byte 3. Check for overflow. Store the result.

We could ignore the overflow flag when adding bytes 1 and 2. Overflow tells us the sign bit is no longer reliable and bytes 1 and 2 have no sign bit.

Subtract and Subtract with Carry

In a subtract operation the value of the second operand is subtracted from the contents of the accumulator and the result is left in the accumulator.

Action	Flags	8080 Mnemonic	Z-80 Mnemonic
$A \leftarrow A - s$	C Z V S	SUB s SUI n	SUB s

In a subtract with carry, the second operand and the carry flag are subtracted from the accumulator and the result is left in the accumulator.

Action	Flags	8080 Mnemonic	Z-80 Mnemonic
$A \leftarrow A - s - C$	C Z V S	SBB s SBI n	SBC A,s

	8080 and Z-80									Z-80 only	
	A	B	C	D	E	H	L	(HL)	n	(IX+d)	(IY+d)
Subtract	97	90	91	92	93	94	95	96	D6n	DD96d	FD96d
Subtract with carry	9F	98	99	9A	9B	9C	9D	9E	DEn	DD9Ed	FD9Ed

AND, OR, and XOR

The action of these logical operators has already been discussed in detail in "Bits, Bytes, and Boolean Operators." In each case the result is left in the accumulator. The mnemonics and OP codes are summarized in the following table.

Action	Flags	8080 Mnemonic		Z-80 Mnemonic
AND	C*ZPS	ANA	s	AND s
		ANI	n	
OR	C*ZPS	ORA	s	OR s
		ORI	n	
XOR	C*ZPS	XRA	s	XOR s
		XRI	n	

*The carry flag is reset by all logical operations.

	8080 and Z-80									Z-80 only	
	A	B	C	D	E	H	L	(HL)	n	(IX+d)	(IY+d)
AND	A7	A0	A1	A2	A3	A4	A5	A6	E6n	DDA6d	FDA6d
OR	B7	B0	B1	B2	B3	B4	B5	B6	F6n	DDB6D	FDB6d
XOR	AF	A8	A9	AA	AB	AC	AD	AE	EEn	DDAEd	FDAEd

Compare Instruction

The compare operation is a subtraction with the answer thrown away. The second operand is subtracted from the contents of the accumulator, but the accumulator is left unchanged. Only the flags are affected.

Compare A: 17
s: 7

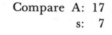

Flag settings:
- C: 0, no carry
- Z: 0, not a zero result
- V: 0, no overflow
- S: 0, positive result

result
discarded

Compare A: 7
s: 17

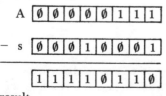

Flag settings:
- C: 1, borrow generated
- Z: 0, not a zero result
- V: 0, no overflow
- S: 1, negative result

result
discarded

The above examples illustrate that if we know for sure that the numbers compared are both positive and both less than 128, then we know

$$A < s \text{ if } S = 1 \text{ (negative result)}$$
$$A = s \text{ if } Z = 1 \text{ (zero result)}$$
$$A > s \text{ if } S = \emptyset \text{ and } Z = 1 \text{ (positive nonzero result)}$$

Similarly, the flag setting for $\leq$, $\geq$, and $\neq$ can easily be determined.

Now suppose we interject the possibility of negative numbers in the compare.

$$A: -7$$
$$s: \quad 7$$

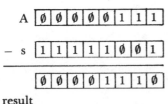

A | 1 | 1 | 1 | 1 | 1 | Ø | Ø | 1 |

$-$ s | Ø | Ø | Ø | Ø | Ø | 1 | 1 | 1 |

| 1 | 1 | 1 | 1 | Ø | Ø | 1 | Ø |

result
discarded

Flag settings:
- C: Ø, no borrow generated
- Z: Ø, not a zero result
- V: Ø, no overflow
- S: 1, negative result

$$A: \quad 7$$
$$s: -7$$

A | Ø | Ø | Ø | Ø | Ø | 1 | 1 | 1 |

$-$ s | 1 | 1 | 1 | 1 | 1 | Ø | Ø | 1 |

| Ø | Ø | Ø | Ø | 1 | 1 | 1 | Ø |

result
discarded

Flag settings:
- C: 1, borrow occurred
- Z: Ø, not a zero result
- V: Ø, no overflow
- S: Ø, positive result

Again it appears that the flag settings discussed for positive numbers will work. But suppose we try to compare 127 and -127. This certainly makes sense.

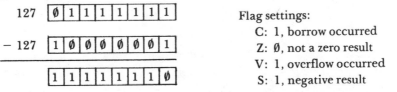

127 | Ø | 1 | 1 | 1 | 1 | 1 | 1 | 1 |

$-$ 127 | 1 | Ø | Ø | Ø | Ø | Ø | Ø | 1 |

| 1 | 1 | 1 | 1 | 1 | 1 | 1 | Ø |

Flag settings:
- C: 1, borrow occurred
- Z: Ø, not a zero result
- V: 1, overflow occurred
- S: 1, negative result

Now if we try to say that $127 < -127$ because the sign bit indicates a negative, we are obviously talking nonsense. Does this mean then that we cannot compare two numbers that we cannot subtract? If so, that would impose a serious restriction on our ability to perform comparisons.

A little analysis reveals the answer. The overflow flag is set when the sign bit is clobbered. If the sign bit has been clobbered, it's just the opposite of what we want for our test.

If $V = \emptyset$ then
$\qquad S = \emptyset \Longrightarrow A \geq s$
$\qquad S = 1 \Longrightarrow A < s$
If $V = 1$ then
$\qquad S = \emptyset \Longrightarrow S$ should really be 1 so $A < s$
$\qquad S = 1 \Longrightarrow S$ should really be $\emptyset$ so $A \geq s$

That's a lot of testing and it looks like it could turn into a lot of code. Now suppose we perform an XOR (exclusive OR) between the overflow and sign flags and compare the result to the chart above.

V	S	V XOR S	Results from Chart Above
1	1	$\emptyset$	$A \geq s$
1	$\emptyset$	1	$A < s$
$\emptyset$	1	1	$A < s$
$\emptyset$	$\emptyset$	$\emptyset$	$A \geq s$

We can now see that

$$(V \ XOR \ S = \emptyset) \Longrightarrow A \geq s$$
$$(V \ XOR \ S = 1) \Longrightarrow A < s$$

We know we can get $A > s$ by taking $A \geq s$ and weeding out the case where $A = s$. So now we can relate all the relationships between A and s to the corresponding flag settings. Flag settings for a comparison of eight bit signed numbers are:

Relationship	Holds if	Comment
$A < s$	V XOR S = 1	
$A \leq s$	V XOR S = 1	$\left(\begin{array}{c} A < s \\ or \\ A = s \end{array} \right)$
	or	
	Z = 1	
$A = s$	Z = 1	
$A \neq s$	Z = $\emptyset$	
$A > s$	V XOR S = $\emptyset$	$\left(\begin{array}{c} A \geq s \\ and \\ A \neq s \end{array} \right)$
	and	
	Z = $\emptyset$	
$A \geq s$	V XOR S = $\emptyset$	

We're still not through discussing the compare operation. What if the values in A and s are not signed numbers? Instead of $-128 \leq A \leq 127$, we have $\emptyset \leq A \leq 255$. That would certainly be a valid interpretation of the eight bits. Such a representation would be especially useful for counting. If, say, we wanted to repeat a certain sequence of instructions 150 times, we may want to compare our current count to this limit. How then shall we interpret the flag settings?

Clearly the zero flag will still work for us. But now the sign and overflow flags have no significance. It is the carry flag that will fill the gap. The carry flag is set whenever a subtraction generates a borrow out of the register.

$$(C = 0) \Longrightarrow A \geq s$$
$$(C = 1) \Longrightarrow A < s$$

No sign bit means no overflow worries, so this chart is easy. The flag settings for a comparison of eight bit unsigned numbers are

Relationship	Holds if	Comment
$A < s$	$C = 1$	
$A \leq s$	$C = 1$ *or* $Z = 1$	$\begin{pmatrix} A < s \\ or \\ A = s \end{pmatrix}$
$A = s$	$Z = 1$	
$A \neq s$	$Z = 0$	
$A > s$	$C = 0$ *and* $Z = 0$	$\begin{pmatrix} A \geq s \\ and \\ A \neq s \end{pmatrix}$
$A \geq s$	$C = 0$	

With the compare operation fully analyzed, it's time to consider the compare instruction. The action of a compare is described as $(A - s)$ since it is based on a subtraction operation. The fact that neither operand is affected in the process is reflected in the absence of an arrow.

Action	Flags	8080 Mnemonic	Z-80 Mnemonic
$(A - s)$	C Z V S	CMP s CPI n	CP s

	8080 and Z-80									Z-80 only	
	A	B	C	D	E	H	L	(HL)	n	(IX+d)	(IY+d)
Compare	BF	B8	B9	BA	BB	BC	BD	BE	FEn	DDBEd	FDBEd

Increment and Decrement Instructions

All of the arithmetic and logical instructions we have seen so far have dealt with two operands, at least one of which was in the accumulator. By contrast, increment and decrement instructions have one operand and it can be contained in one of the following registers.

8080	Source	Z-80
r	Any eight bit register	r
M	The memory location pointed to by the HL pair	(HL)
d(X)*	An indexed memory location	(IX + d)
d(Y)*		(IY + d)

*TDL Z-80

Again, any one of these will be referred to as s.

An increment adds one to the operand. A decrement subtracts one.

Action	Flags	8080 Mnemonic	Z-80 Mnemonic
s←s + 1	Z V S	INR s	INC s
s←s − 1	Z V S	DCR s	DEC s

	8080 and Z-80								Z-80 only	
	A	B	C	D	E	H	L	(HL)	(IX+d)	(IY+d)
Increment	3C	04	0C	14	1C	24	2C	34	DD34d	FD34d
Decrement	3D	05	0D	15	1D	25	2D	35	DD35d	FD35d

Operations on A and F

Complement Accumulator

Complement is another logical operation. It differs from AND, OR, and XOR in that it has only one operand. The complement operation is a 1's complement of the value, so every zero bit is changed to a one, and every one to a zero. Often called a NOT operation, the complement can be summarized in the following truth table.

A	NOT A
1	0
0	1

The NOT operation is repeated bit by bit for every bit in the accumulator.

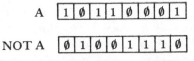

A | 1 | Ø | 1 | 1 | Ø | Ø | Ø | 1 |

NOT A | Ø | 1 | Ø | Ø | 1 | 1 | 1 | Ø |

Complementing the accumulator does not affect any of the flags we have discussed so far. The OP code is 2F. The mnemonics are.

CMA   (8Ø8Ø)
CPL   (Z-8Ø)

Negate Accumulator

The Z-8Ø has an instruction which allows the accumulator to be negated (2's complement).

Action	OP Code	Flags	TDL Z-8Ø and Z-8Ø
A ← – A	ED 44	C Z V S	NEG

8Ø8Ø programmers can substitute for NEG, since 2's complement is 1's complement plus 1.

CMA
INR A

Complement and Set Carry Flag

The carry flag is the only flag which can be directly manipulated. Choices include

Action	OP Code	8Ø8Ø Mnemonic	Z-8Ø Mnemonic
C NOT C	3F	CMC	CCF
C 1	37	STC	SCF

Missing is the ability to reset the carry. The easiest way to reset the carry is to set it and then complement it. But there is a method which is twice as fast. You will recall that any logical operation (except NOT) clears the carry, but the logical operations affect the accumulator's contents unless the second operand is also the accumulator. Clearly, two operations exist which clear the carry and leave the accumulator intact. These are

8Ø8Ø	Z-8Ø
ANA A	AND A
ORA A	OR A

Either of them makes a fine "clear carry flag" instruction.

NOP Instruction

An oddity in the 8080 and Z-80 instruction repertoire is the NOP. With an OP code of 00, the NOP has the distinction of being the instruction that does nothing. The ability to "do nothing" with a particular byte of code can prove very valuable at times, especially during the debugging process.

16 Bit Arithmetic Instructions

There are no 16 bit logical instructions, and only a limited number of arithmetic operations possible. 8080 programmers are limited to increment, decrement, and addition. Increment and decrement can be performed on 16 bit registers BC, DE, HL, and SP. In 16 bit addition, register pair HL acts as the accumulator. The other operand in the addition operation may be registers BC, DE, HL, or SP.

The Z-80 programmer has more choices. The increment and decrement instructions can be applied also to the IX and IY index registers, and other add and subtract operations are possible. It is not possible, however, to add the IX or IY index register to the HL pair. So, before we discuss the Z-80 extensions, let's summarize the instructions the two microprocessors have in common.

To the 8080 programmer rr will mean any one of B for the BC register pair, D for the DE pair, H for HL, or SP for the stack pointer. TDL Z-80 will also include X for the IX index register and Y for the IY register.

To the Z-80 programmer rr will mean any one of BC, DE, HL, SP, IX, or IY.

Action	Flags	8080 Mnemonic	Z-80 Mnemonic
HL←HL + rr	C	DAD rr	ADD HL,rr
rr←rr + 1	none	INX rr	INC rr
rr←rr − 1	none	DCX rr	DEC rr

Note that since the overflow and sign flags are not set, 16 bit operations must be handled carefully.

	8080 and Z-80				Z-80 only	
	BC	DE	HL	SP	IX	IY
ADD	09	19	29	39	—	—
Increment	03	13	23	33	DD23	FD23
Decrement	0B	1B	2B	3B	DD2B	FD2B

Z-80 Extensions

The Z-80 instruction set also includes an add with carry and subtract with carry that treat the HL as an accumulator. Again, the second operand may be in registers BC, DE, HL, or SP. No pure subtract for 16 bit registers exists, though the carry may first be cleared to achieve the equivalent of a pure subtract.

Action	Flags	TDL Z-80 Mnemonic	Z-80 Mnemonic
HL←HL + rr + c	C Z V S	DADC rr	ADC HL,rr
HL←HL + rr − C	C Z V S	DSBC rr	SBC HL,rr

	Z-80 only			
	BC	DE	HL	SP
Add with carry	ED4A	ED5A	ED6A	ED7A
Subtract with carry	ED42	ED52	ED62	ED72

There are also Z-80 extensions which allow the IX and IY registers to act in the role of accumulator.

Action	Flags	OP Code	TDL Z-80 Mnemonic	Z-80 Mnemonic
IX←IX + BC	C	DD09	DADX B	ADD IX,BC
IX←IX + DE	C	DD19	DADX D	ADD IX,DE
IX←IX + SP	C	DD39	DADX SP	ADD IX,SP
IX←IX + IX	C	DD29	DADX X	ADD IX,IX
IY←IY + BC	C	FD09	DADY B	ADD IY,BC
IY←IY + DE	C	FD19	DADY D	ADD IY,DE
IY←IY + SP	C	FD39	DADY SP	ADD IY,SP
IY←IY + IY	C	FD29	DADY Y	ADD IY,IY

Exercises

1. Write a sequence of instructions that will sum a small array of three numbers. The first number is pointed to by the HL pair, and the other two occupy the following two bytes of memory. (You may assume no overflow will occur.)

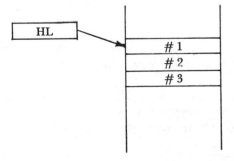

2. Write a sequence of instructions that would add BC and HL, leaving the result in HL. (Assume 16 bit addition is not possible.)

3. A talent agency has discovered it can keep all the information needed about the abilities of its clients in a single byte according to the following scheme.

Bit 7 — 1 Can dance
            Ø Can't dance

Bit 6 — 1 Can sing
            Ø Can't sing

Bit 5 — Can Act
            Ø Can't act

Bit 4 — 1 Does dramatic roles
            Ø Does not

Bit 3 — 1 Does comic roles
            Ø Does not

Bit 2 — 1 Is exceptionally attractive
            Ø Is not

Bit 1 — 1 Has experience
            Ø Has none

Bit Ø — 1 Female
            Ø Male

One such byte is in the accumulator. Tell what instruction will determine if the person involved is a male, singer-dancer, who can act, does both comic and dramatic roles, is experienced, but not exceptionally attractive. What flag will contain the answer?

4. What flags will tell you if A < s and A is

         a.   a signed eight bit number
         b.   an unsigned eight bit number

5. There is no 16 bit compare instruction. Suppose two 16 bit signed variables BIGA and BIGB must be compared. Describe in words a method to accomplish this.

6. The 8080 programmer has no 16 bit subtract. Write a sequence of instructions that will accomplish the subtraction (if overflow can be ignored) of register pairs BC and HL. Leave the result in HL.

4

jumps, loops, and modular programming

In the previous chapter we spent a good deal of time talking about the interpretation of the flag settings after a compare. As yet, however, we have said nothing about how to access the flags and read their values. Flag settings are accessed by means of conditional statement. That is, a command to do something if and only if a flag has a certain value. The instruction to be performed can be a jump or a subroutine call.

Jump Instructions

The normal sequence of program execution is to perform each instruction in turn from top to bottom. The following pattern is continuously repeated.

1. Fetch the instruction.
2. Increment the program counter.
3. Execute the instruction.

A jump instruction alters the normal top-down flow. During execution of the jump instruction (step 3) the address in the program counter is altered. Now, when the next instruction is fetched, it is taken from a different place in the program. So, the instruction to jump to location nn can be diagrammed as

$$PC \leftarrow nn$$

The mnemonics and OP code are

OP Code	8080 Mnemonic	Z-80 Mnemonic
C3 nn	JMP nn	JP nn

Consider the following sequence of instructions.

8080	Z-80
SUB A	SUB A
LXI H,ARRAY	LD HL,ARRAY
SPOT: ADD M	SPOT: ADD A, (HL)
INX H	INC HL
JMP SPOT	JP SPOT

43

The accumulator is cleared and register pair HL is set to point to the starting address of an array in memory. This is the initialization phase of the loop. The contents of the array location pointed to by the HL pair is added to the accumulator. This is the body of the loop. The HL register pair is increased by one. This is the increment phase of the loop. A jump back to spot closes the loop.

However, something is dreadfully wrong here. There is no means of terminating the loop. Left to its own, it would go on forever. When a condition arises to terminate the loop, the jump back should no longer occur. Suppose in our example we decide that we should only repeat the loop five times. What we now need is a conditional jump. Here's the game plan.

1. Set up in some eight bit register the number as a counter.
2. Every time the loop is repeated, decrement that register.
3. When that register goes to zero, don't jump back again.

So what we need is an instruction that performs the following action.

$$\text{If } Z = 0, \text{ PC} \leftarrow nn \text{ (jump on nonzero)}$$

The instruction that will do this for us is

OP Code	8080 Mnemonic	Z-80 Mnemonic
C2 nn	JNZ nn	JP NZ,nn

Now we can rewrite the sequence of instructions to add the first five elements in the array.

```
              8080                    Z-80

              SUB A                   SUB A
              LXI H,ARRAY             LD  HL,ARRAY
              MVI B,5                 LD  B,5
       SPOT:  ADD M            SPOT:  ADD A, (HL)
              INX H                   INC HL
              DCR B                   DEC B
              JNZ SPOT                JP  NZ,SPOT
               .                       .
               .                       .
               .                       .
```

This loop can be broken up into four distinct phases. These four phases will be present in every properly constructed loop:

1. Initialization
2. Body

3. Increment
4. Test

If the four phases appear in the code in the above order, the loop is called a post-test loop. A pre-test loop will contain these phases in the following order.

1. Initialization
2. Test
3. Body
4. Increment

A loop of this form to perform our array sum would be more difficult to construct, since we cannot rely on our decrement to set the zero flag on the first pass. In fact, most pre-test loops will be harder to code in a lower level language. There is, though, a reason for their existence. Consider the following diagrams.

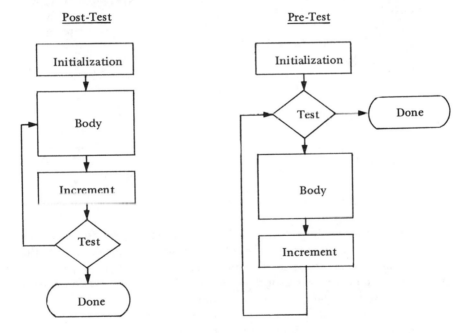

Post-Test   Pre-Test

Now consider the shortest route to Done for each:

Post-Test	Pre-Test
1. Initialization	1. Initialization
2. Body	2. Test
3. Increment	3. Done
4. Test	
5. Done	

Notice that in the post-test loop the body of the loop is always performed at least once. In the pre-test loop, it is possible to avoid performing the loop at all. This then will be the criterion for selecting between the two:

> If there is ever a case where the loop should not be performed at all, use pre-test.

Here is an example of a pre-test loop to add the first five elements of an array:

8Ø8Ø	Initialization	Z-8Ø
SUB A		SUB A
LXI H,ARRAY		LD H,ARRAY
MVI B,5		LD B,5
	Test	
SPOT: MOV C,A		SPOT: LD C,A
MOV A,B		LD A,B
CMP Ø		CP Ø
MOV A,C		LD A,C
JZ DONE		JP Z,DONE
	Body	
ADD M		ADD A,(HL)
	Increment	
INX H		INC HL
DCR B		DEC B
JMP SPOT		JP SPOT
DONE: •		DONE: •
•		•
•		•

Some comments about the test phase are in order. We first save the contents of the accumulator in register C. Then we move the count into the accumulator to compare it to Ø. Now, before our conditional jump, we restore the accumulator to the sum of the array. The move operation doesn't affect the flags, so our jump on zero is still valid.

We now have two loops, one pre-test and one post-test, that sum the first five elements of an array. Both terminate properly, but are the results accurate? We have made no test to see if overflow occurred at any point in the series of additions. What we obviously need is a jump on overflow. Recall, however, that the overflow flag is a dual purpose flag. It also serves as the parity flag. Thus there is only one OP code for both. The 8080 assembler provides two different mnemonics for the same OP code, the Z-8Ø only one, so the programmer must himself keep track of the dual use. We can now summarize the jump instructions.

Action	OP Code	8080 Mnemonic	Z-80 Mnemonic
PC←nn	C3 nn	JMP nn	JP nn
IF Z = 1, PC←nn	CA nn	JZ nn	JP Z,nn
IF Z = 0, PC←nn	C2 nn	JNZ nn	JP NZ,nn
IF C = 1, PC←nn	DA nn	JC nn	JP C,nn
IF C = 0, PC←nn	D2 nn	JNC nn	JP NC,nn
IF S = 1, PC←nn	FA nn	JM nn	JP M,nn
IF S = 0, PC←nn	F2 nn	JP nn	JP P,nn
IF P/V = 1, PC←nn	EA nn	JPE nn JO nn	JP PE,nn
IF P/V = 0, PC←nn	E2 nn	JPO nn JNO nn	JP PO,nn

We could then make our loop to sum the array more accurate by inserting after the addition

```
JO      OVFLOW           8080
J       PE,OVFLOW        Z-80
```

where OVFLOW would be an address in our program that does something about the overflow problem. It may just print an error message and terminate the program.

Z-80 Relative Jumps

Let's take another look at the OP code of the jump instruction.

C3 nn

We can see that it takes three bytes to store this instruction. Since an address is two bytes long, it would seem to be impossible to shorten this instruction. Yet it can be done. Remember that the program counter points to the address of the next instruction to be executed. Suppose that instruction will be a jump. It is very likely that the jump will be to an address near where we are currently. If that address is no farther away than -128 to $+127$ bytes, we can express that address as a distance relative to the current location of the program counter. That relative distance will fit in one byte.

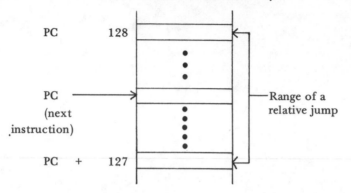

The whole point of the relative jump instructions is this savings in space. Take, for example, our original program rewritten with a relative jump.

	TDL Z-80		Z-80
	SUB A		SUB A
	LXI H,ARRAY		LD HL,ARRAY
SPOT:	ADD M	SPOT:	ADD A,(HL)
	INX H		INC HL
	JMPR SPOT		JR SPOT

The OP code for the relative jump instruction is

$$18\ e$$

where e is the magnitude of the relative jump as a signed number one byte in length.

Ignoring for the moment the fact that this is an infinite loop, let's hand assemble these instructions. Assume ARRAY is located at 3F00 and assume that the program begins at 2000.

Address	Instruction	Action
2000	97	$A \leftarrow A - A$
2001	21003F	$HL \leftarrow 3F00$
2004	86	$A \leftarrow A + (HL)$
2005	23	$PC \leftarrow PC + e$
2006	18e	
2008	•	

What should we use for e? Remember that the sequence of program execution is

1. Fetch the instruction (get 18e).
2. Increment the program counter (PC = 2008).
3. Execute the instruction.

We want to jump to SPOT. SPOT is at location 2004, so we want to solve this little equation:

$$2004 = 2008 + e$$

Clearly e must be –4. In 2's complement:

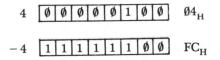

$$4 \quad \boxed{0\;0\;0\;0\;0\;1\;0\;0} \quad 04_H$$

$$-4 \quad \boxed{1\;1\;1\;1\;1\;1\;0\;0} \quad FC_H$$

Thus, at location 2006 in our program we would find

2006: 18FC

Fortunately, all this arithmetic is done for us by the assembler. We need only use the relative jump instruction with the name of the location we want to branch to.

Here, then, are the available relative jump instructions. Only the absolute relative jump, relative jump on carry, and relative jump on zero are provided.

Action	OP Code	TDL Z-80 Mnemonic	Z-80 Mnemonic
PC←PC + e	18 e	JMPR nn*	JR nn
IF Z = 1, PC←PC + e	28 e	JRZ nn	JR Z,nn
IF Z = 0, PC←PC + e	20 e	JRNZ nn	JR NZ,nn
IF C = 1 PC←PC + e	38 e	JRC nn	JR C,nn
IF C = 0, PC←PC + e	30 e	JRNC nn	JR NC,nn

*Here the use of nn indicates the name of the destination.

Z-80 Loop Instruction

There is another relative jump instruction available on the Z-80 that does more than just jump or test and jump. The DJNZ provides the capability of a built-in loop. Its action may be summarized as

$$B \leftarrow B - 1$$
$$\text{if } B \neq 0, \text{ PC} \leftarrow \text{PC} + e$$

The B register must first be set to the number of repetitions desired. Choices range from 1 to 256 repetitions. By setting B to 1-255, the corresponding number of repetitions are achieved. If B is initially set to 0, the first decrement will leave B set to 255, so a total of 256 repetitions will occur before B gets back to 0 again.

Let's repeat the loop that will sum the first five array elements.

	TDL Z-80		Z-80
	SUB A		SUB A
	LXI H,ARRAY		LD HL,ARRAY
	MVI B,5		LD B,5
SPOT:	ADD M	SPOT:	ADD A,(HL)
	INX H		INC HL
	DJNZ SPOT		DJNZ SPOT

The OP code for the decrement-jump-nonzero instruction 10 e.

Register Indirect Jumps

The register indirect jump which the 8080 and Z-80 have in common can be diagrammed as

$$\text{PC} \leftarrow \text{HL}$$

That is, the address in the HL register pair becomes the address where the next instruction will come from. The OP code and mnemonics are

OP Code	8080 Mnemonic	Z-80 Mnemonic
E9	PCHL	JP (HL)

So the following instruction sequences are equivalent

	8080		Z-80
A.			
	•		•
	•		•
SPOT:	•	SPOT:	•
	JMP SPOT		JP SPOT

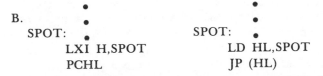

B.
```
      •                        •
      •                        •
SPOT: •                  SPOT: •
      •                        •
   LXI H,SPOT               LD HL,SPOT
   PCHL                     JP (HL)
```

At first sight the E9 one byte OP code would seem to be a great one byte jump. These examples indicate, however, that its true cost is four bytes. Three bytes are taken up by getting the address into the HL register.

Needless to say, this is not the most common form of a jump. Its main value lies in code that must be capable of running at any address whatsoever without requiring any modification. Such code is called self-relocating code. Besides the use of the HL register pair for this purpose, Z-80 programmers may also use the IX or IY registers.

Action	OP Code	TDL Z-80 Mnemonic	Z-80 Mnemonic
PC←IX	DDE9	PCIX	JP (IX)
PC←IY	FDE9	PCIY	JP (IY)

Subroutines and Modular Programming

When a programmer is faced with any nontrivial task, he is well advised to divide the task into individual modules or subroutines. In this regard we can honestly say that no programming assignment is ever difficult. If a task seems formidable break it down into smaller tasks, each of which can be easily handled.

If a task seems too big . . .

just break it up . . .

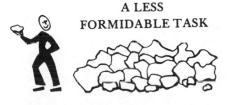

A LESS
FORMIDABLE TASK

and deal with the pieces one by one.

This is modular programming or structured programming. Besides making your life easier when you code the program, it makes the program far easier to understand. Modularity can save space and programming effort if sequences of instructions that must be repeated are written as subroutines (program modules).

Subroutine calls are so easy on the 8080 and Z-80 that we can recommend their use wholeheartedly to the earliest beginner to assembly language programming. The basic instruction used to transfer control to a subroutine is

CALL nn   8080 and Z-80

To get back, the basic instruction is

RET   8080 and Z-80

We can diagram the flow of control as follows.

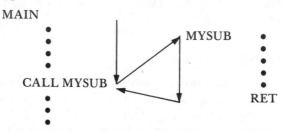

A CALL is like a jump with one difference. The return address is saved on the stack. The return instruction pops the stack and jumps back to the address left there.

That's all there is to it. CALL to get there. RET to get back. Everything needed is done automatically.

You can also nest subroutine CALLs. That is, a subroutine can call a subroutine of its own, and that subroutine can call another subroutine, and so on. The nature of the stack is such that the return addresses will never get mixed up. The program can always find its way back.

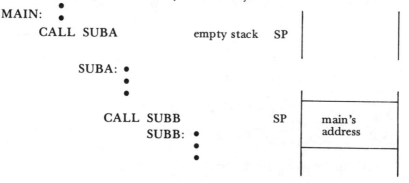

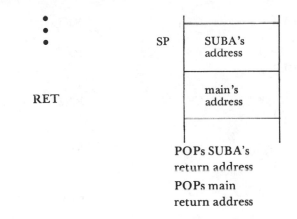

```
    •
    •
    •

                RET


    RET
```

Calls to subroutines and returns from subroutines can be made conditional on the setting of a flag. The instructions are nearly identical to the conditional jumps. They are

Action	OP Code	8Ø8Ø Mnemonic	Z-8Ø Mnemonic
CALL nn	CD nn	CALL nn	CALL nn
If Z = 1, CALL nn	CC nn	CZ nn	CALL Z,nn
If Z = Ø, CALL nn	C4 nn	CNZ nn	CALL NZ,nn
IF C = 1, CALL nn	DC nn	CC nn	CALL C,nn
If C = Ø, CALL nn	D4 nn	CNC nn	CALL NC,nn
If S = 1, CALL nn	FC nn	CM nn	CALL M,nn
IF S = Ø, CALL nn	F4 nn	CP nn	CALL P,nn
IF P/V = 1, CALL nn	EC nn	CPE nn	CALL PE,nn
If P/V = Ø, CALL nn	E4 nn	CPO nn CNO nn	CALL PO,nn

RET	C9	RET	RET
If Z = 1, RET	C8	RZ	RET Z
If Z = Ø, RET	CØ	RNZ	RET NZ
If C = 1, RET	D8	RC	RET C
If C = Ø, RET	DØ	RNC	RET NC
If S = 1, RET	F8	RM	RET M
If S = Ø, RET	FØ	RP	RET P
If P/V = 1, RET	E8	RPE RO	RET PE
If P/V = Ø, RET	EØ	RPO RNO	RET PO

The only complication possible in modular programming involves the use of the registers. Most times both the main program and the subroutine would like full use of the registers. How can the subroutine use all of the registers without messing up their contents for the main program? The answer is simple. The subroutine need only PUSH all of the register values onto a stack, do its thing, and then POP the original contents back in before returning to the main program.

Exercises

1. Suppose VARA and VARB are two unsigned, one byte variables, and the following instruction sequence is executed.

8Ø8Ø	Z-8Ø
LDA VARA	LD A,(VARA)
LXI H,VARB	LD HL,VARB
CMP M	CP (HL)

Write a sequence of instructions that will branch to SPOT if

    a. VARA < VARB
    b. VARA ≤ VARB
    c. VARA = VARB
    d. VARA ≠ VARB
    e. VARA ≥ VARB
    f. VARA > VARB

2. Repeat exercise 1 if VARA and VARB are signed numbers.
3. Write a subroutine which accepts as inputs

    a. the address of an array in a variable named ARYADR
    b. the number of elements in the array in a variable named SIZE

and produces the following outputs.

    a. The sum of all of the array elements left in the accumulator, if no overflow is produced
    b. if overflow occurs, the value 1 left in the variable named OVFLAG. The value returned in the accumulator may be assumed to be meaningless.

No registers except the AF pair may be altered upon return to the main program.

4. Two 16 bit unsigned variables occupy memory locations BIGA and BIGB. Write a sequence of instructions that will call a routine named ABIGR if BIGA ≥ BIGB, and BBIGR if BIGA < BIGB.
5. Repeat exercise 4 if BIGA and BIGB are 16 bit signed variables.
6. For this exercise refer to exercise 3 in the section "A Method To Our Logic." In addition to the assumptions made in that exercise, assume further that the agency keeps the information about its clients in the following form.

Location	Descriptive byte	Jump address
PEOPLE	1	1
PEOPLE + 3	2	2
PEOPLE + 6	3	3
PEOPLE + 9	4	4
⋮	⋮	⋮

The array is named PEOPLE. For each client in the array, there is a descriptive byte and the address of a segment of code that prints out that person's name, address, phone number, etc. The variable named COUNT contains the number of clients currently being serviced. Write a segment of code that will look for the type of person described in the previously mentioned exercise 3. If such a person is found, control should pass to the jump address for the person. If no such person is contained in PEOPLE, the subroutine named NOSUCH should be called.

5

bit fiddling and message making

How can the Z-80 programmer manipulate single bits of data? How do you rotate registers and why would you want to? How are alphabetic characters stored in computer memory? How do you get data into and out of the computer? These are just some of the questions that will be answered in this chapter.

Z-80 Bit Manipulation Instructions

The Z-80 has the capability of testing, setting, or resetting individual bits within a byte. The bits are numbered from low order to high order.

```
7  6  5  4  3  2  1  0
┌──┬──┬──┬──┬──┬──┬──┬──┐
│  │  │  │  │  │  │  │  │
└──┴──┴──┴──┴──┴──┴──┴──┘
```

The byte whose bits are being manipulated may be located in any one of the following areas, any one of which will be referred to as s.

TDL Z-80	Location	Z-80
r	Any eight bit register	r
M	The memory location pointed to by the HL pair	(HL)
d(X)	An indexed memory location	(IX + d)
d(Y)		(IY + d)

The bits in byte s will be referred to by number. The letter b will be used to stand for any bit number 0-7. Thus,

$$s \ \{b\}$$

refers to any bit in any of the above locations.

The bit test instruction sets the zero flag to the opposite of the bit value. Worded differently, the bit test instruction sets the zero flag if the bit has a zero value and resets it otherwise. Diagrammatically,

$$Z \leftarrow \sim s\,\{b\}$$

The mnemonics for both TDL Z-80 and Z-80 are the same.

BIT   b,s

The chart of OP codes is large.

Bit Test

Bit	A	B	C	D	E	H	L	(HL)	(IX+d)	(IY+d)
0	CB47	CB40	CB41	CB42	CB43	CB44	CB45	CB46	DDCBd46	FDCBd46
1	CB4F	CB48	CB49	CB4A	CB4B	CB4C	CB4D	CB4E	DDCBd4E	FDCBd4E
2	CB57	CB50	CB51	CB52	CB53	CB54	CB55	CB56	DDCBd56	FDCBd56
3	CB5F	CB58	CB59	CB5A	CB5B	CB5C	CB5D	CB5E	DDCBd5E	FDCBd5E
4	CB67	CB60	CB61	CB62	CB63	CB64	CB56	CB66	DDCBd66	FDCBd66
5	CB6F	CB68	CB69	CB6A	CB6B	CB6C	CB6D	CB6E	DDCBd6E	FDCBd6E
6	CB 77	CB70	CB71	CB72	CB73	CB74	CB75	CB76	DDCBd76	FDCBd76
7	CB7F	CB78	CB79	CB7A	CB7B	CB7C	CB7D	CB7E	DDCBd7E	FDCBd7E

The bit set instruction sets the indicated bit.

$$s\,\{b\} \leftarrow 1$$

The mnemonics for both TDL Z-80 and Z-80 are again the same.

SET   b,s

Again, there are many OP codes involved.

Bit Set

Bit	A	B	C	D	E	H	L	(HL)	(IX+d)	(IY+d)
0	CBC7	CBC0	CBC1	CBC2	CBC3	CBC4	CBC5	CBC6	DDCBdC6	FDCBdC6
1	CBCF	CBC8	CBC9	CBCA	CBCB	CBCC	CBCD	CBCE	DDCBdCE	FDCBdCE
2	CBD7	CBD0	CBD1	CBD2	CBD3	CBD4	CBD5	CBD6	DDCBdD6	FDCBdD6
3	CBDF	CBD8	CBD9	CBDA	CBDB	CBDC	CBDD	CBDE	DDCBdDE	FDCBdDE
4	CBE7	CBE0	CBE1	CBE2	CBE3	CBE4	CBE5	CBE6	DDCBdE6	FDCBdE6
5	CBEF	CBE8	CBE9	CBEA	CBEB	CBEC	CBED	CBEE	DDCBdEE	FDCBdEE
6	CBF7	CBF0	CBF1	CBF2	CBF3	CBF4	CBF5	CBF6	DDCBdF6	FDCBdF6
7	CBFF	CBF8	CBF9	CBFA	CBFB	CBFC	CBFD	CBFE	DDCBdFE	FDCBdFE

This bit reset instruction resets the indicated bit.

$$s\,\{b\} \leftarrow 0$$

Once again TDL Z-80 and Z-80 mnemonics are the same.

RES   b,s

The OP codes are
Bit Reset

Bit	A	B	C	D	E	H	L	(HL)	(IX+d)	(IY+d)
Ø	CB87	CB80	CB81	CB82	CB83	CB84	CB85	CB86	DDCBd86	FDCBd86
1	CB8F	CB88	CB89	CB8A	CB8B	CB8C	CB8D	CB8E	DDCBd8E	FDCBd8E
2	CB97	CB90	CB91	CB92	CB93	CB94	CB95	CB96	DDCBd96	FDCBd96
3	CB9F	CB98	CB99	CB9A	CB9B	CB9C	CB9D	CB9E	DDCBd9E	FDCBd9E
4	CBA7	CBA0	CBA1	CBA2	CBA3	CBA4	CBA5	CBA6	DDCBdA6	FDCBdA6
5	CBAF	CBA8	CBA9	CBAA	CBAB	CBAC	CBAD	CBAE	DDCBdAE	FDCBdAE
6	CBB7	CBB0	CBB1	CBB2	CBB3	CBB4	CBB5	CBB6	DDCBdB6	FDCBdB6
7	CBBF	CBB8	CBB9	CBBA	CBBB	CBBC	CBBD	CBBE	DDCBdBE	FDCBdBE

Rotate and Shift Instructions

Rotate instructions common to the 8080 and Z-80 microprocessor all involve the accumulator. There are four basic types.

Rotate left circular

Rotate right circular

Rotate left

Rotate right

Action	OP Code	8080 Mnemonic	Z-80 Mnemonic
Rotate left circular	Ø7	RLC	RLCA
Rotate right circular	ØF	RRC	RRCA
Rotate left	I7	RAL	RLA
Rotate right	IF	RAR	RRA

Before we go into those rotate and shift instructions which are exclusively Z-80, let's spend a moment discussing why you might want to rotate a register.

Suppose the accumulator has the following value.

| Ø | Ø | Ø | 1 | Ø | Ø | 1 | Ø | = 18

Then suppose we clear the carry and rotate the accumulator left. It will then contain

| Ø | Ø | 1 | Ø | Ø | 1 | Ø | Ø | $= 36 = 18 \times 2$

Suppose instead we had rotated right. The accumulator would have had

| Ø | Ø | Ø | Ø | 1 | Ø | Ø | 1 | $= 9 = 18 \div 2$

So shift and rotate instructions give us the capability to multiply and divide by powers of two. We are now ready for a generalized algorithm that can be used for multiplication and division in the 8080 and Z-80.

Multiplication and Division

The 8080 and Z-80 microprocessors possess no built-in multiply or divide instructions, so subroutines must be written to provide this capability. We will discuss here algorithms that can be used for positive integers.

The multiplication table for binary numbers isn't long.

$$\emptyset \times \emptyset = \emptyset$$
$$\emptyset \times 1 = \emptyset$$
$$1 \times \emptyset = \emptyset$$
$$1 \times 1 = 1$$

Multiplication of longer numbers is done in the same way as in the decimal system.

```
            1 1 Ø Ø 1 1 1
        ×           1 Ø 1
          ─────────────────
            1 1 Ø Ø 1 1 1
          Ø Ø Ø Ø Ø Ø Ø
        1 1 Ø Ø 1 1 1
        ───────────────────
      1 Ø Ø Ø Ø Ø Ø Ø 1 1
```

Notice that every line in forming the product is either a copy of the multiplicand or all zeroes. The pattern of shifting each row one place to the left is common to decimal multiplication.

Multiplication is notorious for generating large numbers. Assuming both multiplier and multiplicand are one byte signed numbers, how large can the product become? Obviously it's $127^2 = 16,129$. We are way over one byte in length, but well within two bytes. In fact, if we assume multiplier and multiplicand are one byte unsigned numbers the product will still fit in a 16 bit unsigned result. The multiply routine will therefore accept as inputs two one byte signed or unsigned positive integers and produce as output a two byte product of the two.

The method to be used parallels the approach used above. We will need three registers for this operation. One will contain the multiplier, one the multiplicand, and one we will clear for use as a work area.

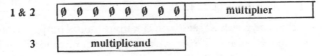

1 & 2 | Ø Ø Ø Ø Ø Ø Ø Ø | multiplier |

3 | multiplicand |

Registers 1 and 2 will be used to contain the result. Register 3 will be left unchanged.

So our example above would begin as

1 & 2 | Ø Ø Ø Ø Ø Ø Ø Ø | Ø Ø Ø Ø Ø 1 Ø 1 |

3 | Ø 1 1 Ø Ø 1 1 1 |

The following two steps will then be repeated eight times.

A. Check bit Ø of register 2 (the multiplier). If it is set, add the contents of register 3 (the multiplicand) to register 1. If the bit is Ø, do not add in the multiplicand. After this step we would have

1 & 2 | Ø 1 1 Ø Ø 1 1 1 | Ø Ø Ø Ø Ø 1 Ø 1 |

3 | Ø 1 1 Ø Ø 1 1 1 |

B. Shift registers 1 and 2 right one bit. At the end of the first iteration we have

| Ø Ø 1 1 Ø Ø 1 1 | 1 Ø Ø Ø Ø Ø 1 Ø |

Continuing this sequence for our sample case gives, on iterations 2–8,

2.A.) No addition
  B.) Shift giving: | Ø Ø Ø 1 1 Ø Ø 1 | 1 1 Ø Ø Ø Ø Ø 1 |

3.A.) Add multiplicand + | Ø 1 1 Ø Ø 1 1 1 |

                 | 1 Ø Ø Ø Ø Ø Ø Ø | 1 1 Ø Ø Ø Ø Ø 1 |

  B.) Shift giving: | Ø 1 Ø Ø Ø Ø Ø Ø | Ø 1 1 Ø Ø Ø Ø Ø |
4.A.) No addition
  B.) Shift giving: | Ø Ø 1 Ø Ø Ø Ø Ø | Ø Ø 1 1 Ø Ø Ø Ø |
5.A.) No addition
  B.)|Shift giving | Ø Ø Ø 1 Ø Ø Ø Ø | Ø Ø Ø 1 1 Ø Ø Ø |
6.A.) No addition
  B.) Shift giving | Ø Ø Ø Ø 1 Ø Ø Ø | Ø Ø Ø Ø 1 1 Ø Ø |

7.A.) No addition
   B.) Shift giving | Ø Ø Ø Ø Ø 1 Ø Ø | Ø Ø Ø Ø Ø 1 1 Ø |
8.A.) No addition
   B.) Shift giving | Ø Ø Ø Ø Ø Ø 1 Ø | Ø Ø Ø Ø Ø Ø 1 1 |

Thus we can see that the result agrees with the long-hand computation.

Division is also extremely simple when the dividend and divisor are in binary. Consider the following example.

$$
\begin{array}{r}
1\emptyset\emptyset\emptyset111 \text{ r } 1\emptyset\emptyset\emptyset \\
11\emptyset1\,\overline{)\,111\emptyset1\emptyset\emptyset\emptyset11} \\
\underline{11\emptyset1} \\
11\emptyset\emptyset\emptyset \\
\underline{11\emptyset1} \\
1\emptyset111 \\
\underline{11\emptyset1} \\
1\emptyset1\emptyset1 \\
\underline{11\emptyset1} \\
1\emptyset\emptyset\emptyset
\end{array}
$$

We knew that in multiplication if we allowed two bytes for a product and restricted inputs to one byte, we could never run into difficulties with overflow. Following that lead, we might decide to use a two byte dividend, a one byte divisor, and expect quotient and remainder to each remain within one byte. But here we are not so lucky. In the above case the dividend will fit within two bytes, but if we divide it by one the quotient will certainly not fit within a byte. So in our division algorithm we will have to be on the lookout for a means of deducing that our result is inaccurate. Again, all inputs will be assumed to be positive integers. We will again need three registers. Registers 1 and 2 will contain the two byte dividend. Register 3 will contain the divisor.

Our example above would begin as

1 & 2 | Ø Ø Ø Ø Ø Ø 1 1 | 1 Ø 1 Ø Ø Ø 1 1 |

3 | Ø Ø Ø Ø 1 1 Ø 1 |

The following three steps will be repeated eight times.

A. Registers 1 and 2 are shifted left one bit.

| Ø Ø Ø Ø Ø 1 1 1 | Ø 1 Ø Ø Ø 1 1 Ø |

B. The contents of register 3 (the divisor) is subtracted from register 1.

1 & 2 | Ø Ø Ø Ø Ø 1 1 1 | Ø 1 Ø Ø Ø 1 1 Ø |

3 | Ø Ø Ø Ø 1 1 Ø 1 |

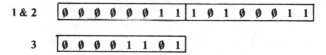

1 & 2 | 1 1 1 1 1 Ø 1 Ø | Ø 1 Ø Ø Ø 1 1 Ø |

C. If the result of the subtraction causes a negative number to result in register 1, the divisor is added back. If not, bit 0 of register 2 is changed to A 1. In this case, a negative result occurred, so we add the divisor back getting the same contents as after step A

Following our example through to the end gives

2.A.) Shift left:

| 0 0 0 0 1 1 1 0 | 1 0 0 0 1 1 0 0 |

B.) Subtract:

− | 0 0 0 0 1 1 0 1 |

| 0 0 0 0 0 0 0 1 | 1 0 0 0 1 1 0 0 |

C.) Set bit 0:

| 0 0 0 0 0 0 0 1 | 1 0 0 0 1 1 0 1 |

3.A.) Shift left:

| 0 0 0 0 0 0 1 1 | 0 0 0 1 1 0 1 0 |

B.) Subtract:

− | 0 0 0 0 1 1 0 1 |

| 1 1 1 1 0 1 1 0 | 0 0 0 1 1 0 1 0 |

C.) Add back:

| 0 0 0 0 0 0 1 1 | 0 0 0 1 1 0 1 0 |

4.A.) Shift left:

| 0 0 0 0 0 1 1 0 | 0 0 1 1 0 1 0 0 |

B.) Subtract:

− | 0 0 0 0 1 1 0 1 |

| 1 1 1 1 1 0 0 1 | 0 0 1 1 0 1 0 0 |

C.) Add back:

+ | 0 0 0 0 0 1 1 0 | 0 0 1 1 0 1 0 0 |

5.A.) Shift left:

| 0 0 0 0 1 1 0 0 | 0 1 1 0 1 0 0 0 |

B.) Subtract:

− | 0 0 0 0 1 1 0 1 |

| 1 1 1 1 1 1 1 1 | 0 1 1 0 1 0 0 0 |

C.) Add back:

+ | 0 0 0 0 1 1 0 0 | 0 1 1 0 1 0 0 0 |

6.A.) Shift left:

| 0 0 0 1 1 0 0 0 | 1 1 0 1 0 0 0 0 |

B.) Subtract:

− | 0 0 0 0 1 1 0 1 |

| 0 0 0 0 1 0 1 1 | 1 1 0 1 0 0 0 0 |

C.) Set bit 0:

| 0 0 0 0 1 0 1 1 | 1 1 0 1 0 0 0 1 |

7.A.) Shift left:

| ∅ | ∅ | ∅ | 1 | ∅ | 1 | 1 | 1 | 1 | ∅ | 1 | ∅ | ∅ | ∅ | 1 | ∅ |

B.) Subtract:

− | ∅ | ∅ | ∅ | ∅ | 1 | 1 | ∅ | 1 |

| ∅ | ∅ | ∅ | ∅ | 1 | ∅ | 1 | ∅ | 1 | ∅ | 1 | ∅ | ∅ | ∅ | 1 | ∅ |

C.) Set bit ∅:

| ∅ | ∅ | ∅ | ∅ | 1 | ∅ | 1 | ∅ | 1 | ∅ | 1 | ∅ | ∅ | ∅ | 1 | 1 |

8.A.) Shift left:

| ∅ | ∅ | ∅ | 1 | ∅ | 1 | ∅ | 1 | ∅ | 1 | ∅ | ∅ | ∅ | 1 | 1 | ∅ |

B.) Subtract:

− | ∅ | ∅ | ∅ | ∅ | 1 | 1 | ∅ | 1 |

| ∅ | ∅ | ∅ | ∅ | 1 | ∅ | ∅ | ∅ | ∅ | 1 | ∅ | ∅ | ∅ | 1 | 1 | ∅ |

C.) Set bit ∅:

| ∅ | ∅ | ∅ | ∅ | 1 | ∅ | ∅ | ∅ | ∅ | 1 | ∅ | ∅ | ∅ | 1 | 1 | 1 |

At the conclusion of the division operation we have

1 & 2 | Remainder | Quotient |

A check of our original example shows that we obtained the correct answer.

But what about our potential overflow? If we had begun with the dividend used in the previous example, but made the divisor the number 1, we know the result would overflow. But how would we know this happened?

A complicated chain of reasoning will reveal an extremely simple test. We want to trap the quotients that won't fit in one byte. The largest signed number that will fit is $+127$. So we want to know about it whenever

$$\frac{\text{Dividend}}{\text{Divisor}} \geq 128$$

or

$$\text{Dividend} \geq 128 \times \text{Divisor}$$

or

$$\frac{\text{Dividend}}{128} \geq \text{Divisor}$$

So a first try might be to divide the dividend by 128 and compare. Fortunately $128 = 2^7$ so we can do this by shifting right seven bits. Let's try this on our sample case and see what we get.

Before: | ∅ | ∅ | ∅ | ∅ | ∅ | ∅ | 1 | 1 | 1 | ∅ | 1 | ∅ | ∅ | ∅ | 1 | 1 |

After: | ∅ | ∅ | ∅ | ∅ | ∅ | ∅ | ∅ | ∅ | ∅ | ∅ | ∅ | ∅ | ∅ | 1 | 1 | 1 |

We lost all the contents of the high order byte. This will always be true whenever a positive number is input. So we only have one byte left. Compare it to the contents of the high order byte, if we shift one bit to the left.

Ø	Ø	Ø	Ø	Ø	1	1	1	Ø	1	Ø	Ø	Ø	1	1	Ø

We can see that they match. What has this gotten us?

In the first step of the division algorithm, we shift one bit to the left. We have seen that the high order byte then contains

$$\frac{Dividend}{128}$$

In the second step of the algorithm we subtract the divisor from the high order byte.

$$\frac{Dividend}{128} \geq Divisor$$

Here is our compare. It is done in the normal course of the algorithm!

Now notice that the third step of the algorithm has us setting bit Ø if the result of the subtraction was not a negative number. So if the bit is set it means

$$\frac{Dividend}{128} \quad Divisor \quad or \quad \frac{Dividend}{128} > Divisor \quad Ø$$

This is exactly the overflow we were looking for.

Now a second try emerges. Simply check the first iteration. If the subtract step doesn't produce a negative result, we're headed for overflow. Before we decide on this method, though, let's see what happens to this bit. At the end of the first iteration it is set, so the result contains

1 & 2	xxxxxxxx	xxxxxxx1

Seven more iterations remain. With each iteration that bit will be shifted one place to the left. Thus at the end of the algorithm it will appear as

1 & 2	xxxxxxxx	1xxxxxxx

Right in the sign bit itself!

The final result of all this analysis couldn't be simpler:

A negative result indicates overflow.

We know that if dividend and divisor are both positive the result will always be positive. So this gives us an unfailing check.

Z-80 Rotate and Shift Instructions

In all of the rotate instructions we have discussed so far, the location of the operand was always the accumulator. The Z-80, however, permits rotation and shifts of operands located in any of the following areas

TDL Z-80	Location	Z-80
r	Any eight bit register	r
M	The memory location pointed to by the HL pair	(HL)
d(X)	An indexed memory location	(IX + d)
d(Y)		(IY + d)

Any of these locations will be referred to as s. The possible types of rotations are the same as those for the accumulator.

Action	TDL Z-80 Mnemonic	Z-80 Mnemonic
Rotate left circular	RLCR s	RLC s
Rotate right circular	RRCR s	RRC s
Rotate left	RALR s	RL s
Rotate right	RARR s	RR s

OP codes are as follows.

	A	B	C	D	E	H	L	(HL)	(IX+d)	(IY+d)
Rotate left circular	CB07	CB00	CB01	CB02	CB03	CB04	CB05	CB06	DDCBd06	FDCBd06
Rotate right circular	CB0F	CB08	CB09	CB0A	CB0B	CB0C	CB0D	CB0E	DDCBd0E	FDCBd0E
Rotate left	CB17	CB10	CB11	CB12	CB13	CB14	CB15	CB16	DDCBd16	FDCBd16
Rotate right	CB1F	CB18	CB19	CB1A	CB1B	CB1C	CB1D	CB1E	DDCBd1E	FDCBd1E

Besides these extended rotate instructions, the Z-80 possesses the capability to perform shifts on any of the locations s described above. The possible shift instructions are

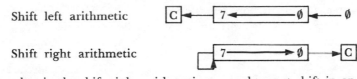

Shift left arithmetic

Shift right arithmetic

Notice that in the shift right arithmetic a zero does not shift in on the left. Instead, the sign bit is repeated to preserve the sign of the number. A pair of examples should make this clear. In each assume that the carry flag was initially cleared.

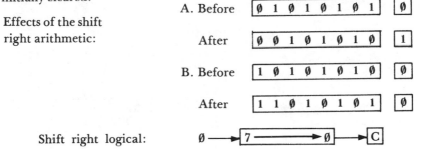

Effects of the shift right arithmetic:

A. Before

After

B. Before

After

Shift right logical:

Notice that no shift left logical is needed, since it would not be any different than a shift left arithmetic.

The mnemonics are

Action	TDL Z-8∅ Mnemonic	Z-8∅ Mnemonic
Shift left arithmetic	SLAR s	SLA s
Shift right arithmetic	SRAR s	SRA s
Shift right logical	SRLR s	SRL s

The OP codes are

	A	B	C	D	E	H	L	(HL)	(IX+d)	(IY+d)
Shift left arithmetic	CB27	CB2∅	CB21	CB22	CB23	CB24	CB25	CB26	DDCBd26	FDCBd26
Shift right arithmetic	CB2F	CB28	CB29	CB2A	CB2B	CB2C	CB2D	CB2E	DDCBd2E	FDCBd2E
Shift right logical	CB3F	CB38	CB39	CB3A	CB3B	CB3C	CB3D	CB3E	DDCBd3E	FDCBd3E

Two final rotate instructions available in the Z-8∅ are of great use in binary coded decimal (BCD) arithmetic. Although this forms the subject of a later chapter, the instructions will be presented here for completeness. The TDL Z-80 and Z-80 mnemonics are identical. The operands are always the contents of the accumulator and the memory location pointed to by the HL pair.

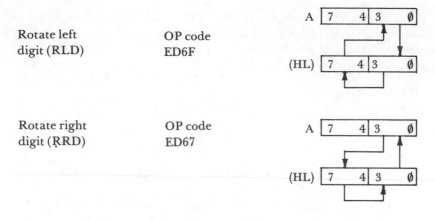

| Rotate left digit (RLD) | OP code ED6F |
| Rotate right digit (RRD) | OP code ED67 |

Character Representation Using the ASCII Code

We have already seen that a byte of memory may have many uses. It can contain an instruction OP code or a piece of data, part of an address or an immediate within an instruction. We will see now that a byte may also contain the coded representation for a character.

What if a programmer wishes to store customer names in memory? Since he has only numbers to deal with, some type of correspondence between letters and numbers must arbitrarily be made. The ASCII code is the most common code used in microcomputers. It is basically a seven bit code, though many systems use the high order bit to signal a graphics character. A complete chart of ASCII is included for reference in Appendix B. Notice that there is a character 1 which in ASCII is hexadecimal 31.

All input from the keyboard and output to screen or printer is usually done in ASCII code. Once in the machine, characters can be stored in ASCII or converted to some other convenient form. For example, suppose we read in the number 123. In character form this is 313233_H and occupies three bytes. To use this as a value within our program we will have to convert it to binary. After conversion it will fit into a byte.

Notice that ASCII contains representations for both A and a.

$$A = 41$$
$$a = 61$$

Many printers can only handle upper case. Any lower case letter can be converted to upper case by subtracting 20_H. This is often referred to as folding to upper case.

Whether the programmer will have to write little utility routines to convert to binary and back again or to fold characters to upper case will depend on the kind of work he is doing. Nearly all programs, however, require some sort of I/O (input/output).

A check of the instruction repertoire of the 8080 will reveal some nice input and output instructions, but the casual programmer will never use them: The monitor generally performs all I/O for the user. Although this arrangement is a tremendous convenience for the user, it is a tremendous headache for the instructor and for the novice programmer. There is no standard, set way of doing I/O. Monitors differ in both techniques of use and range of options. The simplest output technique requires the user to place a single character in a given eight bit register and call a routine that displays or prints it. Input under such a system is also a call to a fixed routine. Upon return, the character input can be found in a given eight bit register.

Exercises

1. Write a subroutine that will accept as inputs two eight bit positive numbers located in variables named MLTPLR and MLTCND. The routine should multiply them and output a two byte result in a variable named PRODCT. Save any registers used by the subroutine.

2. Repeat exercise 1 if MLTPLR and MLTCND cannot be assumed to be positive. (Hint: Test first. Complement each if necessary. Complement result if necessary. For the multiply itself, call the routine in exercise 1.)

3. Write a routine which will accept as inputs a two byte variable named DIVDND and a one byte variable named DIVSOR. (Both may be assumed to be positive.) The routine should divide DIVDND by DIVSOR and output the one byte quotient and remainder in variables named QOTENT and RMANDR, respectively. If an overflow occurs, set RMANDR to a flag value of -1.

4. For this exercise, refer to exercise 6 in "Jumps, Loops, and Modular Programming." Write a subroutine that will sort the array PEOPLE into two arrays called WOMEN and MEN. Keep track of how many elements are in each array and store those values in suitably named variables.

5. Write a subroutine that will accept as inputs the two byte address of an array of characters in a variable named WHERE and the number of characters in a variable named DIGITS. All of the characters should be the ASCII code of *binary* digits, i.e.,

$$0 = 30_H$$
$$1 = 31_H$$

The subroutine should convert the character string into a single binary number and leave its value in a two byte memory location named RESULT.

6. Repeat exercise 5 using

    a. all characters hexadecimal digits
    b. all characters decimal digits

(Hint: You may want to call the multiply or divide routines already written.)

7. Repeat exercises 5 and 6, going the other way. That is, accept a two byte RESULT in binary, output the characters in the array, and store the number of digits required in DIGITS.

8. Learn how I/O is handled through the monitor on your system.

6

a casual introduction
to data structures

Up to now we have referred to variables as things which somehow already were in existence. We blithely said things like "Assume BIGA and BIGB are 16 byte variables in memory." Yet we have never hinted at how they got there. By now we are used to writing instructions in mnemonic form and letting the assembler convert them to OP codes and addresses. We will do basically the same thing for variable declaration, but the mnemonics used to reserve space for variables depend on the individual assembler you are using. The most common choices are to

1. Declare a one byte storage area and assign it an initial value.

   LILVAR: .BYTE 77

2. Declare a two byte storage area and assign an initial value.

   BIGVAR: .WORD 777

3. Reserve a stated number of bytes of storage with no initial values assigned to them.

   ARRAY: .BLKD 7

   (In this example we get 7 bytes of storage reserved. Only the first byte has a name.)

It would be a good idea for you to take the time right now to find out what key words your assembler wants you to use in reserving space for your variables.

Using the Single Variable

A single variable, whether one byte or two bytes in length, can be accessed directly through its name.

8Ø8Ø	Z-8Ø
LDA LILVAR	LD A,(LILVAR)
LHLD BIGVAR	LD HL,(BIGVAR)

71

The Array

We have already made several references to arrays, drawing on previous experience and the context to provide meaning. Basically, whenever there was more than one of anything, we called it an array. To be more accurate, an array is a collection of like items. Usually only the first element of the array is named. So our sample array from example C above would appear as

(1)	1023
(2)	1024
(3)	1025
(4)	1026
(5)	1027
(6)	1028
(7)	1029

ARRAY ⟶

In higher level languages, we would typically access the elements by sub-scripting.

ARRAY(3)

But in assembly language we would have to write

ARRAY + 2

to get the correct address in memory. The trick is getting used to counting:

Typical arrays are dealt with in loops. For example, we can add one to the value of every element in an array. If the individual elements are single bytes, this probably only requires setting up the start address in the HL pair and looping through the array.

Multi-Dimensional Arrays

Suppose we wish to represent in computer memory an array that is, say, 4 × 5. It is convenient for us to think of our storage as a block

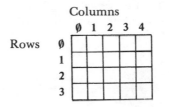

even though the bytes are arranged linearly in memory, what must be done before this can be accomplished is to decide on what order the elements should appear in memory. There are two most likely choices.

	0	1	2	3	4
0	Ø	1	2	3	4
1	5	6	7	8	9
2	1Ø	11	12	13	14
3	15	16	17	18	19

A. Row major order

	0	1	2	3	4
0	Ø	4	8	12	16
1	1	5	9	13	17
2	2	6	1Ø	14	18
3	3	7	11	15	19

B. Column major order

Locating a specific box will depend on the choice of representation used.

Row major order
Box # — col. # + (row #) * (total # of cols.)

Column major order
Box # = row # + (col. #) * (total # of rows)

This whole concept can be extended to three- and four-dimensional arrays when needed.

The Structure

Closely allied to the concept of the array is the structure. Where an array is a collection of like items, a structure is a collection of items which are not necessarily alike.

For example, consider a collection of customer entries:

CUSTNO	NAME	ADDRSS	PHONE

|←— 7 bytes —✻— 20 bytes —✻— 30 bytes —✻— 7 bytes →|

Here a whole customer entry is 64 bytes long. (This turns out to be a very convenient size.) So if we have a pointer to the start of one entry and we want to get to the next we need only add 64. The individual fields of the entries are all fixed displacements from the start of the entry.

Field	Displacement
CUSTNO	0
NAME	7
ADDRSS	27
PHONE	57

Most assemblers allow the programmer to write an equate statement. That is, to create a word that can be used in place of a number. Again, the key word to do this varies from assembler to assembler.

$$TWO = 2$$

or

$$TWO\ EQU\ 2$$

Once an equate has been written, the assembler will translate all references to it to the appropriate value. The use of equates adds greatly to the readability of the program.

Getting around in a structure always involves using these displacements, so it is a prime candidate for the indexed instructions which the Z-80 offers. Suppose the IX index register points to one of the customer entries. We can put the first letter of the customer's name into the C register with

TDL Z-80	Z-80
MOV C,NAME(X)	LD C,(IX + NAME)

(Assuming, of course, that we first wrote an equate statement telling the assembler that by the word "NAME" we really mean the number 7).

Do you see how much clearer the above instruction is than the following?

MOV C,7(X)	LD C,(IX + 7)

This is the beauty of an equate.

8080 programmers must perform an addition to achieve the desired result. Suppose the HL pair points to one of the customer entries. We can put the first letter of the customer's name into the C register with

PUSH	H	Save original pointer
LXI	D,NAME	Displacement value in DE
DAD	D	Add in _placement
MOV	C,M	Get first letter of name

The task takes a little longer without the indexing capability.

Achieving Variable Displacement in the Index Instructions

The Z-80 index instructions always involve a fixed, signed displacement d. Oftentimes a programmer may desire to have the displacement vary. Variable displacement can be achieved as follows.

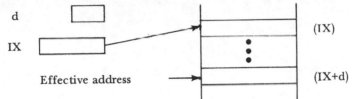

Suppose we wish to access locations of varying displacement from a table which begins at hexadecimal location 137B. We know that the effective address of an index instruction is the contents of the IX index register plus the fixed displacement. If, for example, the displacement were 5

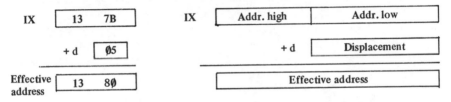

Now we know we always want the same starting location for the table, but we want to vary the displacement. So let's switch things around a little. First, notice that we get the same effective address with

IX	13	05		IX	Addr. high	Displacement
+ d		7B		+ d		Addr. low
	13	80				Same effective address

But here the variable part is in the IX index register where we can get at it to change it, while the table address that never changes anyway is in the fixed d.

We will shortly summarize the program steps that will accomplish this goal, but first we have to take a close look at what we have here. Remember that the displacement d is a signed number ($-128 \leq d \leq 127$), but the low order byte of an address is an unsigned number ($0 \leq$ addr. low < 256). So suppose we tried the same switch using a table that starts at 13FF and a desired displacement of 5.

The $FF_H = -1$, so $1305 - 1 = 1304$ would be used as the effective address, though it is hardly the desired result.

The solution centers around the concept of boundary alignment and the 256 byte page. The first address in any microcomputer is 0000_H; the last is $FFFF_H$. Memory can be considered to be divided into 256 byte pages as follows.

0000 ⋮ Page 0 00FF	The start address of any page of memory is of the form
0100 ⋮ . Page 1 01FF	XX00
0200 ⋮ Page 2 02FF	So the high order address byte can be anything, but the low order address byte is always 00, for any address that is aligned on an even page boundry.

etc.

Forcing this boundary alignment is sometimes essential. The means by which this is accomplished is the origination or location statement. The key word used is again dependent on the assembler, but ORG and LOC are common.

$$.LOC\ 1000_H$$

This would set the next location declared to hexadecimal address 1000.

If we wish to use variable displacement to access an array named TABLE, we need to make use of a reference location we call TBASE, which is aligned on an even page boundary. TABLE itself may lie anywhere in the range TBASE -128 to TBASE $+127$. The distance between TABLE and TBASE will then be a one byte signed number. We use this d as the fixed displacement called for in the index instruction. We use the high order byte of TBASE as the high order portion of the index register. The variable displacement forms the low order portion of the index register. This variable displacement will now be an unsigned number in the range 0 to 255.

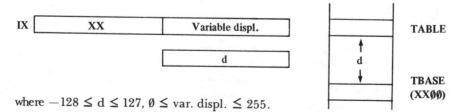

where $-128 \leq d \leq 127$, $0 \leq$ var. displ. ≤ 255.

With the object clearly in mind, there remains only one question. How do we get a one byte variable displacement into the low order half of the index register? The answer is that we plan ahead and reserve for ourselves a two byte area to which we have given the value TBASE (XX00).

INDEX: .WORD TBASE

Now the value of TBASE will be stored in memory in swapped form.

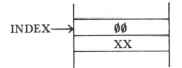

Then suppose our variable displacement is contained in the one byte memory location named DISPL. The following sequence of instructions will set up the IX index register.

TDL Z-80		Z-80	
LDA	DISPL	LD	A, (DISPL)
STA	INDEX	LD	(INDEX),A
LIXD	INDEX	LD	IX,(INDEX)

Linked Structures

All other data structures we have discussed so far have been sequential in nature. That is, the elements have been located physically one after the other in memory. Now we will briefly introduce a type of data structure where the elements may be physically scattered. The individual elements in such a structure are often called nodes. In such a data structure each element will contain the address where the next element can be found. This is often referred to as the link field. If our customer structure were organized this way, it might look like

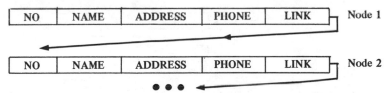

In this case it would no longer be necessary to add 64 to get the next customer. We need only load the value of the link. Typically a link value like 0000 could be used to indicate the end of the list.

One obvious advantage of using a linked structure comes when the individual structure elements must be arranged in a certain order. For example, suppose our customer structure is alphabetized by customer name. (For convenience, only the name field is used.)

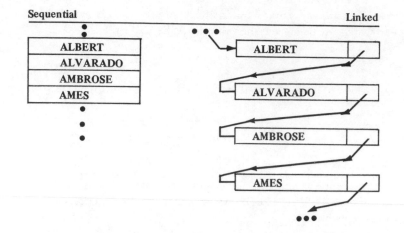

Immediately we can see that the linked representation takes more room, but not much more. An address in an 8080 or Z-80 is two bytes long. So our link fields will add two bytes to every node. But the nodes were already 64 bytes long, so as a percentage the increase is not great.

Suppose, though, that we now acquire a new customer named AMBLE. Using the sequential method, we will have to move every entry down to make room for the new one. With the linked representation we need only change ALVARADO's link to point to AMBLE and have AMBLE's link point to AMBROSE.

Available Nodes List

When linked structures are used, it is convenient to keep a separate list of unused nodes.

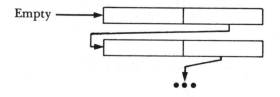

Then when a new entry is needed, we can take the node from this list. Similarly, when we wish to delete an existing node from the linked structure, we can return it to this list to be reused at a later time.

Z-80 Block Handling Instructions

The Z-80 instruction set contains eight operations that act on blocks of data. Whole arrays can be moved or searched using a single command. We will outline the effects of the instructions and then discuss how these instructions might influence the way we chose to store arrays using the Z-80.

Z-80 Block Transfer Group

The Z-80 Block transfer instructions make use of three register pairs:

BC: Holds the count telling how many bytes are to be moved.
DE: Points to the destination location to which the next byte will be moved.
HL: Points to the source location from which the next byte will be fetched.

The load and increment instruction LDI moves one byte from (DE) to (HL) and then increments both DE and HL and decrements register pair BC. The dual purpose flag parity/overflow is set if BC $\neq$ 0 and it is cleared if BC = 0. The carry flag is unaffected, but the zero and sign flags are messed up. The OP code for this instruction is EDA0.

The load, increment, and repeat instruction LDIR performs the same action as the LDI, but continues transferring bytes one by one until the count in the BC register pair reaches zero. It's OP code is EDB0.

The load and decrement instruction LDD moves one byte from (DE) to (HL) and then decrements all three register pairs. Flag settings are the same as for the LDI. The OP code is EDA8.

The load, decrement, and repeat instruction LDDR performs the LDD until the BC pair goes to 0. Its OP code is EDB8.

Z-80 Block Search Group

The Z-80 block search instructions make use of two register pairs and the accumulator.

A: Holds the value to be searched for.
BC: Holds the count telling how many bytes are to be searched.
HL: Points to the location of the next byte to be searched.

The flag settings for these instructions are all the same.

CARRY:	Unaffected.
ZERO:	Set if A = (HL). Cleared if A $\neq$ (HL).
PARITY/ OVERFLOW:	Set if BC $\neq$ 0. Cleared if BC = 0.
SIGN:	Messed up.

The compare and increment instruction CPI performs a compare [A−(HL)]; then increments the HL pair and decrements the BC pair. The OP code is EDA1.

The compare, increment, and repeat instruction CPIR performs the action of the CPI instruction until either BC ≠ Ø, or A = (HL). Its OP code is EDB1.

The compare and decrement instruction CPD performs a compare [A−(HL)], then decrements both the HL and BC register pairs. The OP code is EDA9.

The compare, decrement, and repeat instruction CPDR performs the action of the CPD instruction until either BC = Ø or A = (HL). Its OP code is EDB9.

Z-8Ø Array Arrangement

Suppose we are writing a program that requires a large array of two byte signed variables which are not sorted in any particular order.

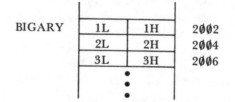

Further, suppose that we frequently have to determine whether or not a certain two byte variable, called TSTVAL, is contained within BIGARY. If all of these variables were one byte in length, there would be no problem. We would simply use the search instruction. However, there is no two byte search. We can still use the built-in search, though, if we split up the array into two arrays of one byte variables.

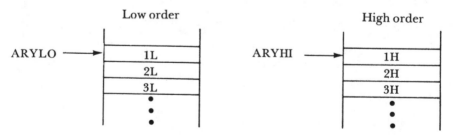

We would also conceptually divide TSTVAL into a high and low order byte. Now we can search just the low order byte for a match with TSTVAL/low. If we find one, we check the corresponding high order byte for a match with TSTVAL/high. If they match, we're done, if not, we just go on checking the low order byte array.

Many times it will turn out to be simpler to split the fields of a structure in this manner as well. In our customer structure, for example, it may be more convenient to keep several parallel arrays.

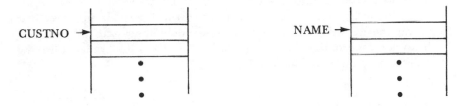

Exercises

1. When an array contains a string of characters that is being input or output a character at a time, it is usually called a buffer. Using the keywords that your assembler requires to reserve storage, define a buffer large enough to hold 30 characters. Write a subroutine that will accept a string of characters from the keyboard and place them in successive buffer locations. The input should be terminated by a carriage return, but do not include that character in the buffer. Clear any unused buffer locations by inserting the ASCII character for a space. Do not allow the buffer to overflow. Each character input should be echoed on the screen or printer.

2. Write a subroutine which will display a message on the screen or printer. The routine should be passed a starting location of the message and the number of characters.

3. Write a driver routine that calls the subroutines written in exercises 1 and 2 above. It should display the following three questions in turn, and accept a response for each.

    NAME?
    ADDRESS?
    PHONE NUMBER?

    The driver should have storage areas reserved for the answers and should transfer the information from the buffer after each question. The area reserved for phone number should be eight characters long. Name and address may be any suitable length up to 30 characters.

4. When using a linked structure, the available nodes list keeps the track of unused nodes. Suppose we have a linked structure where the nodes are 64 bytes long, and where the first two bytes contain the link field.

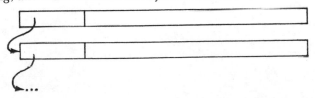

Reserve an area of storage which is 1k (400_H) in length. Force boundary alignment so that it begins on an even page boundary.

a. Write a subroutine that will link up all of the storage space into one big available nodes list. Leave a pointer to the first node in a two byte variable named AVAIL. The last node should have a zero link value.
b. Write a subroutine that will get a node off from the available list and return a pointer to it in the HL pair.

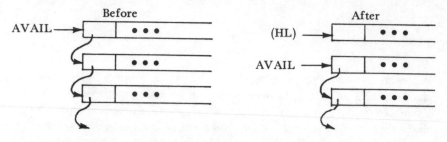

Your routine should check to see if the available nodes list is empty and should call a routine called OVFLOW if it is.

c. Write a subroutine that will accept a pointer to a node in the HL pair and return that node to the available nodes list. That is, reverse "before" and "after" pictures of part b.

7

binary coded
decimal arithmetic

From previous exercises, we have gained experience writing conversion subroutines that accept as input ASCII characters of digits and produce as output the binary equivalent of the number. For example, an input in characters of 11 would be converted to a binary 1011, since

$$11_D = 1011_B$$

Then, if we were to store that number in an eight bit register, it would appear as

0	0	0	0	1	0	1	1

If we were to store the decimal number 11 in binary coded decimal, however, it would appear in a register as

0	0	0	1	0	0	0	1

In binary coded decimal arithmetic, each decimal digit is translated into binary and stored in half a byte (one nibble). So only the following binary values are used.

$$0000 = 0$$
$$0001 = 1$$
$$0010 = 2$$
$$0011 = 3$$
$$0100 = 4$$
$$0101 = 5$$
$$0110 = 6$$
$$0111 = 7$$
$$1000 = 8$$
$$1001 = 9$$

The binary numbers below are not used.

$$1010 = A$$
$$1011 = B$$
$$1100 = C$$
$$1101 = D$$
$$1110 = E$$
$$1111 = F$$

So if we now consider the largest number that will fit in the accumulator, we see that it is

$$\boxed{\text{1} \quad \emptyset \quad \emptyset \quad \text{1} \mid \text{1} \quad \emptyset \quad \emptyset \quad \text{1}}_{\text{BCD}} = 99_{\text{D}}$$

Now 99 isn't a very large number, especially in light of financial applications which use an implied decimal point. If dollars and cents are the units, our 99 becomes 99¢. — this is terribly limiting. Nor does use of a 16 bit register help much — with it we can only go up to $99.99.

The desired size range for BCD numbers can only be achieved by storing the numbers in memory and manipulating them in memory as well. Thus, a BCD number will appear as an array of bytes in memory, each byte containing two digits.

$$1,256,743.27 =$$

$\emptyset$1
25
67
43
27

Notice that only the digits themselves appear in memory, not the decimal point. The fact that two digits follow the decimal point will be contained in a descriptor block which will also give the size of the number in bytes and the sign of the number, whether positive or negative.

Decimal Adjust Instruction

Suppose we decided to add two BCD numbers. For convenience, let's suppose each number is exactly two digits long.

$$\begin{array}{r} 19 \\ + \ 23 \\ \hline 42 \end{array}$$

Now let's see what we would get in the accumulator if we performed addition on these two numbers in BCD.

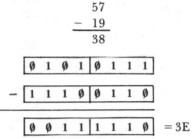

Whoops! The result of this addition left us with one of the unused binary numbers, namely C = 1100. So we added two BCD numbers, but the result was not a BCD number.

We would have a similar problem upon performing the following subtraction:

$$
\begin{array}{r}
57 \\
- \ 19 \\
\hline
38
\end{array}
$$

| 0 | 1 | 0 | 1 | 0 | 1 | 1 | 1 |

− | 1 | 1 | 1 | 0 | 0 | 1 | 1 | 0 |

| 0 | 0 | 1 | 1 | 1 | 1 | 1 | 0 | = 3E

So how can we add or subtract BCD numbers? The answer comes in the form of an additional instruction. The decimal adjust instruction DAA, OP code 27, takes a result in the accumulator, such as the 3C from the above addition, and automatically corrects it to the value 42. The same instruction also corrects the outcome of a subtraction operation.

Multi-byte addition and subtraction algorithms will be given later. Now that we know we can successfully add and subtract BCD numbers, let us turn our attention to conversions between character and BCD forms of the numbers.

Input and Output of BCD Numbers

We know that BCD numbers will be stored in memory with two digits per byte, but the same numbers will be input and output in character form. For example, if the number 1234 were input from the keyboard it would appear in the input buffer in character form. Then it would have to be "packed" into BCD form as illustrated below.

| 31 | 32 | 33 | 34 |

| 12 | 34 |

Similarly, on output, conversion would have to go the other way.

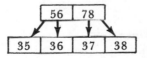

Let's consider how this conversion might be done. From character to BCD

1. Load the first digit into the accumulator. A $\boxed{0\ 0\ 1\ 1\ |\ 0\ 0\ 0\ 1}$ = 31_H

2. Subtract 30_H.   A $\boxed{0\ 0\ 0\ 0\ |\ 0\ 0\ 0\ 1}$ = 01_H

3. Rotate the accumulator four times to the left.   A $\boxed{0\ 0\ 0\ 1\ |\ 0\ 0\ 0\ 0}$ = 10_H

4. Save this value in a temporary storage location.   B $\boxed{0\ 0\ 0\ 1\ |\ 0\ 0\ 0\ 0}$

5. Load the second digit into the accumulator.   A $\boxed{0\ 0\ 1\ 1\ |\ 0\ 0\ 1\ 0}$ = 32_H

6. Subtract 30_H.   A $\boxed{0\ 0\ 0\ 0\ |\ 0\ 0\ 1\ 0}$ = 02_H

7. Add in the value from the temporary storage location.   A $\boxed{0\ 0\ 0\ 0\ |\ 0\ 0\ 1\ 0}$ = 02_H

8. Save the result as the first byte of the BCD number.   +B $\boxed{0\ 0\ 0\ 1\ |\ 0\ 0\ 0\ 0}$ = 10_H

     $\boxed{0\ 0\ 0\ 1\ |\ 0\ 0\ 1\ 0}$ = 12_H

The above steps would be repeated for each pair of characters input. Converting from BCD to character

1. Load the first byte of the BCD number into the accumulator. $\boxed{0\ 1\ 0\ 1\ |\ 0\ 1\ 1\ 0}$ = 56_H

2. Perform an "AND" operation with a mask whose value is $F0_H$.   A $\boxed{0\ 1\ 0\ 1\ |\ 0\ 1\ 1\ 0}$ = 56_H

     AND mask $\boxed{1\ 1\ 1\ 1\ |\ 0\ 0\ 0\ 0}$ = $F0_H$

     $\boxed{0\ 1\ 0\ 1\ |\ 0\ 0\ 0\ 0}$ = 50_H

3. Rotate the accumulator to the right four times.   A $\boxed{0\ 0\ 0\ 0\ |\ 0\ 1\ 0\ 1}$ = 05_H

4. Add in 30_H A $\boxed{0\ 0\ 1\ 1\ |\ 0\ 1\ 0\ 1}$ = 35_H

5. Output the result as the first digit in character form.

6. Load the first byte of the BCD number into the accumulator again. $\boxed{0\ 1\ 0\ 1\ |\ 0\ 1\ 1\ 0}$ = 56_H

7. Perform an "AND" operation with a mask whose value is $0F_H$.   A $\boxed{0\ 1\ 0\ 1\ |\ 0\ 1\ 1\ 0}$ = 56_H

     AND mask $\boxed{0\ 0\ 0\ 0\ |\ 1\ 1\ 1\ 1}$ = $0F_H$

     $\boxed{0\ 0\ 0\ 0\ |\ 0\ 1\ 1\ 0}$ = 06_H

8. Add 30_H and output the result as the second character of the result. $\boxed{0\ 0\ 1\ 1\ |\ 0\ 1\ 1\ 0}$ = 36_H

Again, all eight steps would have to be repeated for each pair of characters output.

RLD and RRD in Character–BCD Conversions

The 8080 programmer has no choice but to use the above algorithm or one equivalent to it. The Z-80 programmer can make use of the RLD and RRD instructions to simplify the conversion routines. These two instructions have been discussed before, but they are diagrammed again here for reference.

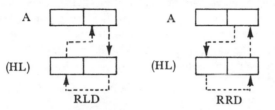

Let's trace how the algorithms would go using these instructions for conversion from character to BCD. Assume the following register pairs are used as pointers.

HL: points to the first character in the input buffer
DE: points to the first byte of the BCD

1. Clear the accumulator and RRD the first digit into the accumulator.

A $\boxed{\emptyset\ \emptyset\ \emptyset\ \emptyset\ |\ \emptyset\ \emptyset\ \emptyset\ \emptyset}$ = 00_H A $\boxed{\emptyset\ \emptyset\ \emptyset\ \emptyset\ |\ \emptyset\ \emptyset\ \emptyset\ 1}$ = 01_H

(HL) $\boxed{\emptyset\ \emptyset\ 1\ 1\ |\ \emptyset\ \emptyset\ \emptyset\ 1}$ = 31_H (HL) $\boxed{\emptyset\ \emptyset\ \emptyset\ \emptyset\ |\ \emptyset\ \emptyset\ 1\ 1}$ = 03_H

Before   After

2. Store the contents of the accumulator into the location pointed to by the DE pair.

3. Increment the HL pair to point to the next character, and repeat step 1.

A $\boxed{\emptyset\ \emptyset\ \emptyset\ \emptyset\ |\ \emptyset\ \emptyset\ 1\ \emptyset}$

4. Now exchange the contents of the DE and HL registers (DE ⟷ HL) so the HL pair points to the first byte of the BCD number. Then RLD second digit into the byte.

A $\boxed{\emptyset\ \emptyset\ \emptyset\ \emptyset\ |\ \emptyset\ \emptyset\ 1\ \emptyset}$ = 02_H A $\boxed{\emptyset\ \emptyset\ \emptyset\ \emptyset\ |\ \emptyset\ \emptyset\ \emptyset\ \emptyset}$ = 00_H

(HL) $\boxed{\emptyset\ \emptyset\ \emptyset\ \emptyset\ |\ \emptyset\ \emptyset\ \emptyset\ 1}$ = 01_H (HL) $\boxed{\emptyset\ \emptyset\ \emptyset\ 1\ |\ \emptyset\ \emptyset\ 1\ \emptyset}$ = 12_H

Before   After

These four steps can then be repeated for each pair of digits input.

Storing the BCD Number in Memory

We have already stated that a BCD number generally occupies several bytes and requires some type of descriptor block telling

1. size
2. number of digits to the right of the decimal point
3. sign

The method presented below is by no means the only possible way to store this information. Its main advantage is simplicity. The maximum size of the number to be dealt with is completely up to the programmer and will depend on the application. The storage area to be reserved, however, will be three bytes larger than the space required to hold the longest possible number. Those three bytes will then hold the descriptor data for the number.

$$1234.56$$

would appear in memory as

Ø6
Ø2
ØØ
12
34
56

The number is 6 digits long,
two digits to the right of the decimal point, and
the number is positive ($Ø1_H$ indicates negative).

} This is the number itself.

Alignment of the BCD Number

We have still not completely characterized the BCD number. Suppose the following number is input.

$$123.45$$

This number has five digits in it, and we pack two to a byte, so there will be an odd digit left over. Should we store the number as

Ø1
23
45

or

12
34
5Ø

The first method will turn out to be the simplest to deal with, because in this representation the decimal point lies between two bytes and not in the middle of a byte. This will turn out to be extremely useful in addition and subtraction of numbers with decimal points in different places. In fact, we will make it a rule always to have the decimal point on a byte boundary.

123.456

would appear in memory as

Ø1
23
45
6Ø

But now what should we put in the descriptor block? We have just changed both the number of digits in the number and the number to the right of the decimal point. The answer is that we will want to use the descriptor block to tell us the total number of bytes to the right of the decimal point.

Number of bytes in number
Number of bytes to the right of the decimal point
Sign
Value   • • •

Now what about our input routines? We designed them as though the number would simply be read from left to right in the buffer. Now we want to work outward from the decimal point in both directions. Does this mean the whole set of routines will have to be discarded? Fortunately, this will not be necessary if we are careful in the design of our data areas. The algorithm to be used will be outlined, but at this time let us also discuss how to set up the descriptive block and how to deal with extraneous character inputs such as "," or "." or "+".

We will begin by allowing an extra byte of storage whose value is 30_H. This byte will be located just before the buffer area.

SPARE:	.BYTE	30_H
BUFFER:	.BLKB	12Ø
SPRFLG:	.BLKB	1
NUMBER:	.BLKB	65

We will then assume that the number is input into the buffer area beginning at BUFFER + 0. Examination of the buffer contents will thus begin at that address. Each character in the buffer will be examined in turn.

Initialization: Zero the space flag (SPRFLG) and the entire data area reserved for NUMBER. Set the HL and DE register pairs so that both point to BUFFER + 0. Zero registers B + C to be used for counts.

Presignificance loop (repeat 1 and 2 until a jump out of the loop occurs):

1. Fetch a character from the buffer location pointed to by the DE pair.
2. Test for one of the following and perform the corresponding action upon a match:

a. Space — Increment the DE register pair.
   $
   +

b. —   — Move a 1 to the sign descriptor byte. Increment the DE register pair.
c. .   — Increment the DE register pair and jump to the post-decimal loop.
d. Digit — Move the character to the location pointed to by the HL pair.
   (0-9)   Increment both the DE and ·HL registers. Increment the B register. Jump to the post-significance loop.
e. Any   — Jump to the termination segment.
   other

Post-significance loop (repeat 1 and 2 until a jump out of the loop occurs):

1. Fetch a character from the buffer location pointed to by the DE pair.
2. Test for one of the following and perform the corresponding action upon a match:

a. ,   — Increment the DE register pair.
b. —   — Move a 1 to the sign desciptor byte. Jump to the termination segment.
c. .   — Increment the DE register pair and jump to the post-decimal loop.
d. Digit — Move the character to the location pointed to by the HL pair.
   (0-9)   Increment both the DE and HL registers. Increment the B register.
e. Any   — Jump to the termination segment.
   other

Post-decimal loop (perform 1 and then repeat 2 and 3 until a jump out of the loop occurs):

1. Check the digit count in register B. If it is an odd number (bit 0 is set), increment register B and set the spare flag (SPRFLG ← 1).
2. Fetch a character from the buffer location pointed to by the DE pair.

3. Test for one of the following and perform the corresponding action upon a match:

a. — — Move a 1 to the sign descriptor byte. Jump to the termination segment.

b. Digit — Move the character to the location pointed to by the HL pair.
(∅-9) Increment both the DE and HL registers. Increment both the B and C registers.

c. Any — Jump to the termination segment.
other

Termination segment:

1. Check the digit count in register B. If it is an odd number (bit ∅ is set) increment both the B & C registers and move the value 30_H to the location pointed to by the HL pair.

2. Divide the contents of register B by 2 by shifting to the right and store this value in size.

3. Repeat for register C, store in number of digits to the right of the decimal point.

4. Set the HL register pair to point to
   a. BUFFER + ∅ — if SPRFLG = ∅
   b. SPARE — if SPRFLG = 1

5. Use the previously described translation routine to convert the input characters to BCD. The number of repetitions for the loop is the value in SIZE.

Although this routine may seem to be long and complex, it is really worth the effort to encode and debug it. Once written, it becomes a highly portable utility routine that can be used in any application requiring BCD arithmetic.

Fixed Point Addition and Subtraction

We have already seen how the use of the decimal adjust instruction DAA can greatly simplify addition and subtraction of BCD numbers. Now it is time to consider the subleties of decimal point alignment and discuss how a BCD routine to add and subtract fixed point numbers might be structured.

First consider the following addition operation.

$$1.∅23 + 7.7$$

A routine that performs this addition must take into account the need to properly align the decimal point.

$$
\begin{array}{r}
1.∅23 \\
+ \ 7.7 \\
\hline
8.723
\end{array}
$$

It is also necessary to decide on the location for the result of the operation. If it is decided to leave the result in either the first or the second operands, the fact that the result may be larger than the inputs must be taken into account in the algorithm design. Lastly, the routines must take into account the sign of the inputs, since the numbers themselves are not stored in any fashion such as 2's complement which allows them to be dealt with directly.

The routines described below will extend zeroes to the right of the decimal point of the shorter number to solve the alignment problem. For example,

$$1.023 + 7.7$$

will become

$$
\begin{array}{r}
1.023 \\
+\ \ 7.700 \\
\hline
8.723
\end{array}
$$

The location of the result will be a totally separate result area. This area will act as a buffer in the sense that a second call to the addition routine will destroy the result of the previous addition. So the calling program will have to move the result to the location of its choice.

The sign of the inputs will be taken into account in the following manner.

Addition:

Operands of the same sign:	Perform addition on the two operands. Attach their common sign to the result.
Operands of opposite sign:	Subtract the smaller from the larger. Attach the sign of the larger to the result.

Subtraction:

Given operand 1 minus operand 2, change the sign of operand 2 and add. Restore the sign of operand 2 before returning from the subroutine.

The whole subject of attaching the proper sign to the result apparently depends on the ability to compare two BCD numbers. Since these numbers can be extremely long, such a comparison may seem difficult. In fact, it is not terribly hard to do this. Before a comparison is made, the two numbers will first be adjusted so they have the same number of bytes to the right of the decimal point. At this time the size of the two numbers can be compared. If one is longer, it is larger. Numbers of the same length can be subjected to a byte-by-byte unsigned compare.

The routines themselves make use of two length indicators. These are the lengths of the two operands after decimal point adjustment has taken place. The basic loops merely involve a straight add (or subtract) of the lowest order byte and an add (or subtract) with carry of every higher order byte until the shorter number is exhausted. After that point has been reached, the routine continues to add (or subtract) with carry using a "dummy" operand with a zero value until the longer number is exhausted. After each and every ad dition (or subtraction) the decimal adjust operation is performed.

Floating Point Multiplication

The method to be used in floating point multiplication parallels that used in long-hand computation.

$$
\begin{array}{r}
7.032 \\
\times\ \ .42 \\
\hline
14064 \\
28128 \\
\hline
2.95344
\end{array}
$$

The size of the result will be, at most, the sum of the sizes of the two operands. The number of bytes to the right of the decimal point will be exactly the sum of the numbers of bytes to the right of the decimal point in the two operands.

To outline the method to be used, consider the two BCD operands as strings in memory. The smaller operand will be used as the multiplier and will have a pointer to its least significant digit's byte

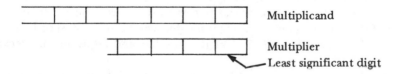

Multiplicand

Multiplier
Least significant digit

The digit in the multiplier will be read, and the multiplicand will be added into the result that many times. The addition will ignore the decimal point in the multiplicand. Then the multiplicand will be shifted to the left four bits (i.e., multiplied by 10), and the next digit in the multiplier will be considered. This process will be repeated until all of the digits of the multiplier have been used up. In the process of left shifting the multiplicand, the RLD instruction will prove invaluable.

The sign of the resulting product can easily be determined by comparing the signs of the operands:

Operands		Result
+	+	+
+	−	−
−	+	−
−	−	+

Floating Point Division

Again the technique utilized will parallel that used in long division. To trace the method, however, we will have to analyze the thought processes used in division very carefully. Consider first the approach taken in performing the following long division.

$$6.347 \overline{\smash{\big)}\ 10.4}$$

The first step in performing this division by hand would be to shift the decimal point three places to the right in both the divisor and the dividend.

$$6.347. \overline{\smash{\big)}\ 10.400.} = 6347 \overline{\smash{\big)}\ 10400.}$$

Once this step has been performed, the decimal point is fixed in the result. But in our algorithm it will be the number of bytes to the left of the decimal point that we will want to keep track of, since the number of bytes to the right will depend on the accuracy with which the calculation is performed. The desired number of bytes of accuracy would have to be input to the subroutine as a parameter.

An outline of the algorithm follows.

1. Check the number of bytes to the right of the decimal point in the divisor. If this is nonzero, multiply both dividend and divisor by 100 by using an eighth bit left shift. Repeat this step until the divisor has no digits to the right of the decimal point. The eight bit shift can be accomplished by simply adding the digits 00 to the end of the number and adjusting the decimal point.

2. Subtract the number of bytes to the right of the decimal point from the total number of bytes to obtain the number of bytes to the left of the decimal point in the dividend.

3. Now create the quotient by performing the following loop the number of times equal to the desired accuracy as input. Note that using this system leading zeroes will be counted as digits of accuracy. The number of bytes of accuracy would be obtained by adding to the end of the dividend the required number of 00 bytes to make its total length equal to the desired accuracy. Begin the loop by left shifting the dividend four bits and taking only the first byte as the assumed size of the dividend.

    a. Subtract the divisor from the assumed size of the dividend. Keeping a count of the number of subtractions performed, repeat until the result goes negative. At that point, add the divisor back and decrement the subtraction count. Output the count as a digit of the quotient.

    b. Left shift the dividend four bits, but maintain the same assumed size of the dividend. Repeat step a.

    c. Left shift the dividend four bits and increase the assumed size of the dividend by one byte. Repeat steps a-c until the desired number of bytes of accuracy have been obtained.

    1. When the entire quotient has been formed, delete leading 00 bytes and adjust the decimal point accordingly.

Exercises

1. Write a subroutine which will take as input a number in character form in a buffer and produce as output the BCD value of the number.
2. Write a subroutine which will perform a fixed point addition of two BCD numbers.
3. Write a subroutine which will perform a fixed point subtraction of two BCD numbers.
4. Write a subroutine which will perform a floating point multiplication of two BCD numbers.
5. Write a subroutine which will perform a floating point division of two BCD numbers.

8

when time is important

In this chapter we will be dealing with two totally separate types of time. On the one hand, we will discuss how to optimize program development time. That is, how to get the most from the human hours that go into program design, coding, testing, and debugging. On the other hand, we will consider how to minimize machine execution time in applications where run speed is critical.

An Approach to Program Development

George has just been given a job contract to develop a complete microcomputer program for a talent agency. He talks to the owner and she spends an hour and half telling him all the things she wants the program to do. The task seems frightening, but he will make enough money to pay for his complete computer system five times over.

At home, perched at his desk and ready to work, he drags out all the notes he took at his interview. The first thing he will want to do is *(1) begin with a clear idea of what the program is to accomplish*. George determines that the talent agency wants the program to maintain a complete, up-to-date file containing name, address, phone number, and abilities profile for each of its clients. The agency would like to give an casting director an immediate yes or no answer as to whether they have a client on file with a given abilities profile. If the director wants to make an interview appointment, the agency will need to get a display of the names, addresses, and phone numbers of all clients who fit the profile. With the total task summarized, George's thoughts are already turning to the second step: *(2) divide the total task into any isolatable sub-tasks*.

He can identify three clearly distinguishable sub-tasks in the talent agency program:

    a. keeping the client file current
    b. performing a search for a given profile
    c. listing name, address, phone on matches

Now George is really clicking, ideas are starting to pour in. He jots down on scratch paper a few ideas he doesn't want to forget. For instance, the thought just occurred to him that all the information the agency needs to know about its people can be contained in a single byte. But George doesn't get carried away from his planning. He moves right into the third step: *(3) concentrating on a single one of the sub-tasks, repeat step 2. Repeat 2 and 3 until all of the program modules have been designed.*

George zeroes in on the problem of keeping the client file current. He divides it as follows.

A. adding new clients and their profiles
B. updating a field in a client record
C. deleting former clients and their profiles

The problem of adding new clients and their profiles becomes the next series of tasks.

i. getting a new node area
ii. filling in name, address, and phone fields
iii. collecting employee profile information and organizing it into a descriptive byte

Getting a new node is no problem. George can easily adapt a subroutine he wrote long ago to do this. Filling in name, address, and phone fields he had also done before. George has a collection of message input and output subroutines to draw on. So the only problem George faces right now is collecting and organizing profile information. Deeply absorbed in his work, George has completely forgotten how awesome the task appeared at first. The profile task still needs narrowing down. He refers to his notes and decides that he can use his standard I/O subroutines to collect the answers to a series of questions. He'll convert a yes to a 1 and a no to a 0. Going into the routine he'll clear the accumulator. Then he'll set the low order bit accordingly and shift one to the left before the next question.

Before too long, and well before the design deadline, George has the complete program design. He knows what his data will look like in memory. He knows what routines and subroutines are needed for the job and has a good idea of what machine capabilities he will utilize in the performance of each task. He has a complete block diagram of his program showing which routines call what subroutines. A portion of George's block diagram is shown on the following page.

Through all this design effort, George has not written a single line of assembly language code. With the design complete, though, he's ready to begin coding. It's no haphazard guess as to what to code first. George is following the fourth step: *(4) code the main driver first, then all first level subroutines and so on, coding from the top down to the lowest level subroutine.* Coding takes a long time. A few problems arise for George, but he discovers that even though he has to adjust his design a little, he never seems to have to make many changes to code he has already written. That's the *top-down* approach working for him. If he'd begun coding from the lowest level subroutine up, he would be spending half his time erasing code and tracking down the repercussions of minor changes.

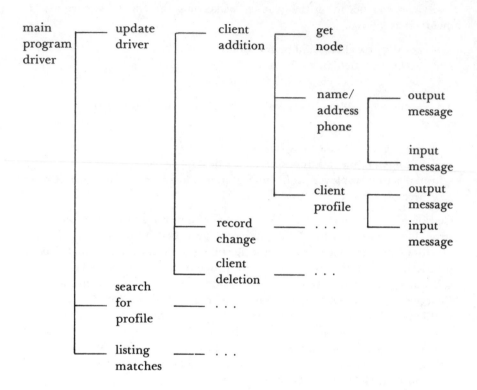

George is doing more than just writing code right now. He is documenting every routine he writes. Long ago he formed the habit of commenting every line of assembly code. SET 5,D won't give you any clues as to what you were up to when you wrote it two weeks ago. But line comments aren't enough for a project of this size. George keeps a whole block of comments as a header to each subroutine. He always includes

NAME:	The complete name of the routine with acronyms expanded in full.
FUNCTION:	A brief description of the purpose of the routine.
CALLED BY:	The names of all the routines that call this routine.
CALLS:	The names of all the routines that this routine calls.
ARGUMENTS:	Any data that is passed to this routine in a register or returned from this routine in a register is clearly spelled out.

George never omits any of these items. For instance, in his main program driver he has the line

CALLED BY: NONE

Then he knows that no item was forgotten. George also carefully documents the data structures he is using. The name, the size, the function, and the alignment of all variables and tables are included.

Finally the job of coding is finished and George surveys the job with satisfaction. The program fills a three ring binder. He has sections separated by dividers for all his documentation and for each subroutine. Now he is ready to begin to assemble the code and test it. George is quite excited about the project. He's itching to enter all the code, assemble it, and let it rip. But he knows that method would only give him a big letdown. Even the smallest subroutine isn't guaranteed to run the first time. It has to be debugged, and with a project of any size, that can be either a nightmare or a smooth, orderly procedure, depending on the way it is approached. So George won't let his enthusiasm run away with him. Instead he'll follow the fifth step: *(5) assemble and test the lowest level subroutines first, working from the bottom up.*

George begins with the utility routines he's adapting from previous programs. His basic I/O routines really get the once-over. Every time George tests a routine, he uses the same basic plan. He is always careful to include test cases that will exercise every branch. He wants to be sure that every line of code is executed during the test phase. When he feels confident that the jumps are jumping properly and the loops are looping, George is still not ready to certify the routine as fully debugged. What if bad data comes through? What if a clerk types a name where a number should have been entered? Will the whole program come to a crashing halt? George has included data validation checks in his subroutine designs wherever a problem could cause a crash. Now, during debug, he will try out the weirdest of the weird data inputs to see what effects they have on the system. If an empty array is passed, will the loop droop? If the program runs out of space for more clients, will it ignore the problem and wipe out anything in its way?

If George discovers that he's done a "jump on zero" when he wanted a "jump on a nonzero" or some such error, he can alter the program.

LOC 204E = CA 4323 (jump on zero to 2343)

George can simply change one instruction by TE at 204E to a D2, so

LOC 204E = D24323 (jump on nonzero)

Such changes are very simple when the corrected instruction is the same length as the original instruction.

If George discovers that he's got an instruction in the program that he doesn't want, he can just substitute NOP instructions in its place. For example, to remove

LOC 214B = CD3750 (call loc. 5037)

replace it with three NOPs:

LOC 214B = 00
      214C = 00
      214D = 00

Now what if George discovers he's forgotten an instruction that should be there? He could stop his debugging in midstream while he corrects the program and reassembles, or he could simply make a "patch." A patch is a program repair that involves making an unconditional jump out to an unused location in memory (called the patch area). There, any omitted instructions can be hand assembled and listed directly in machine code before making an unconditional jump back to program area. There are four steps involved.

1. Create a jump out to the patch area "C3 __ __" by replacing three bytes in the program. [If you replace only part of an instruction, be sure to replace the rest of it with NOP(s).]
2. In the patch area replace the instruction(s) removed for the jump.
3. Enter the missing instruction(s) in machine code.
4. Code a jump back to the program area at the end of the patch.

A patch log which shows all changes to the program made during debug can prove to be invaluable.

Only when he's convinced that the routine is uncrashable does George certify it complete and go on to the next. As new routines are debugged, they are combined with the previous ones, gradually building toward the complete system. When at last the day comes that the driver takes off and drives, George knows he's got a winner. He takes a well-earned couple of days off before the final work on the system.

Yes, there's more. George wants to be sure the program will work under field conditions, so he copies names from the phone book and invents profiles randomly until he has as many "clients" on his system as the agency will have. Will searches slow to unbearable waits under a heavy load? Will an agency clerk give a yes to a casting director only to discover that there's only one client with that profile, and his address and phone number are garbled? George needs to know the answers. Can he do the search if a director says, "I don't care if it's a man, woman, or goat—just send me someone who can act!"

Fortunately, George did his work well and his system responds gracefully to the most outlandish inputs. It's time for a party! But soon after, he's back to work. Still? Yes, George has to write his user documentation. Complete, clear, easy-to-follow directions must be prepared for each type of entry or inquiry to the system. George doesn't assume any knowledge on the part of the operator. He makes the documentation complete enough for the first-time user, but at the same time, concise enough to provide quick reference for the experienced user.

Needless to say, now that George has delivered the completed system to the talent agency, he feels confident that it will serve them well. And George . . . well, he's vacationing in Bermuda.

Optimizing Run Time

It is in pursuit of speed that most programmers turn to assembly language code. The interpretive nature of BASIC slows execution to the point where complex programs run at an intolerably slow pace. For most applications, merely switching to assembly language provides the needed speed up. Occasionally, however, the application is so demanding and so time-critical that the use of assembly code in itself is not enough. In such applications it is necessary to identify those segments of code which must be executed repeatedly within a short time frame, perhaps thousands of repetitions must be made within a minute or so. Once the real bottlenecks have been isolated, these routines can be optimized.

Optimization of code requires an awareness of the time the computer spends in executing a particular type of instruction. The time is not so much the absolute time required for each, but more important, is the relative execution times of the various instructions. We will measure relative execution times in terms of a "T-state." A T-state corresponds to a single clock pulse in the central processing unit. The actual time required for a T-state depends on the clock speed of the individual microprecessor. For instance, if the microprocessor is running at 1 MHz (one megahertz), then there are one million T-states per second. A 4 MHz clock rate produces four million T-states per second.

When trying to decide whether optimization is worthwhile, remember that T-states must be saved by the millions to cut seconds off execution time.

The instruction times for each instruction as measured in T-states are included in the instruction summary appendix. The execution times fall into basic groups depending on the location of the operands. The fastest type of instruction, for instance, operates on two operands which are both located in eight bit registers. The chart on page 102 summarizes the instruction times for eight bit operands based on operand location.

Here we see the characteristic longer execution times for the indexed instructions which typically take 2.5 to nearly 6 times longer than the corresponding instruction in an eight bit register. To show how optimization can take place, suppose the code you were trying to speed up used an indexed storage location to hold a temporary result in a computation. To put the value out in memory would require 19 T-states. To retrieve it, another 19, for a total of 38. Saving the same value in an eight bit register takes four T-states and four to retrieve it, for a total cost of eight T-states. If that register is free, we've found a way to save 30 T-states.

Operation	r	(HL)	n	(IY + d) (IX + d)	(nn)
LOAD ADD SUBTRACT AND OR XOR COMPARE	4	7	7	19	13*
INCREMENT DECREMENT	4	11	—	23	—
ROTATE SHIFT SET BIT RESET BIT	8† 4	15	—	23	—
BIT TEST	8	12	—	20	—

*LOAD only.
†Except accumulator.

Exercise

1. As a programmer, you have now had numerous examples of code written by and for you. You should by now have investigated the I/O techniques used in your monitor and learned the key words your assembler needs to see to locate a program at a fixed spot in memory and to reserve and name storage locations. If you have not already done so, it's time to learn how to create a text file on your system and how to assemble and load a program. We have just finished discussing techniques for organizing an approach to large programming projects. In short, you should now have all the tools necessary to tackle a programming project of your own design.

8080/ZILOG MNEMONICS CONVERSION

SYMBOLS USED

SYMBOL	OPERATION
r	one of the 8-bit registers A,B,C,D,E,H,L
n	any 8-bit absolute value
ii	an index register reference, either X or Y
d	an 8-bit index displacement, where $-128 < d < 127$
zz	B for the BC register pair, D for the DE pair
nn	any 16-bit value, absolute or relocatable
rr	B for the BC register pair, D for the DE pair, H for the HL pair, SP for the stack pointer
qq	B for the BC register pair, D for the DE pair, H for the HL pair, PSW for the A/Flag pair
s	any of r (defined above), M, or d(ii)
IFF	interrupt flip-flop
CY	carry flip-flop
ZF	zero flag
tt	B for the BC register pair, D for the DE pair, SP for the stack pointer, X for index register IX
uu	B for the BC register pair, D for the DE pair, SP for the stack pointer, Y for index register IY
b	a bit position in an 8-bit byte, where the bits are numbered from right to left 0 to 7
PC	program counter
b{n}	bit n of the 8-bit value or register v
vv/H	the most significant byte of the 16-bit value or register vv
vv/L	the least significant byte of the 16-bit value or register vv
Iv	an input operation on port v
Ov	an output operation on port v
w ← v	the value of w is replaced by the value of v
w ↔ v	the value of w is exchanged with the value of v

8 BIT LOAD GROUP

8Ø8Ø MNEMONIC	OPERATION	ZILOG MNEMONIC	# OF BYTES	# OF T STATES
MOV r,r'	r ← r'	LD r,r'	1	4
MOV r,M	r ← (HL)	LD r,(HL)	1	7
MOV r,d(ii)	r ← (ii+d)	LD r,(Iii+d)	3	19
MOV M,r	(HL) ← r	LD (HL),r	1	7
MOV d(ii),r	(ii+d) ← r	LD (Iii+d),r	3	19
MVI r,n	r ← n	LD r,n	2	7
MVI M,n	(HL) ← n	LD (HL),n	2	1Ø
MVI d(ii),n	(ii+d) ← n	LD (Iii+d),n	4	19
LDA nn	A ← (nn)	LD A,(nn)	3	13
STA nn	(nn) ← A	LD (nn),A	3	13
LDAX zz	A ← (zz)	LD A,(zz)	1	7
STAX zz	(zz) ← A	LD (zz),A	1	7
LDAI	A ← I	LD A,I	2	9
LDAR	A ← R	LD A,R	2	9
STAI	I ← A	LD I,A	2	9
STAR	R ← A	LD R,A	2	9

16 BIT LOAD GROUP

8Ø8Ø MNEMONIC	OPERATION	ZILOG MNEMONIC	# OF BYTES	# OF T STATES
LXI rr,nn	rr ← nn	LD rr,nn	3	1Ø
LXI ii,nn	ii ← nn	LD ii,nn	4	14
LBCD nn	B ← (nn+1) C ← (nn)	LD BC,(nn)	4	2Ø
LDED nn	D ← (nn+1) E ← (nn)	LD DE,(nn)	4	2Ø
LHLD nn	H ← (nn+1) L ← (nn)	LD HL,(nn)	3	16
LIXD nn	IX/H ← (nn+1) IX/L ← (nn)	LD IX,(nn)	4	2Ø

8080 Mnemonic	Operation	Zilog Mnemonic	# of Bytes	# of T States
LIYD nn	IY/H ← (nn+1) IY/L ← (nn)	LD IY,(nn)	4	20
LSPD nn	SP/H ← (nn+1) SP/L ← (nn)	LD SP,(nn)	4	20
SBCD nn	(nn+1) ← B (nn) ← C	LD (nn),BC	4	20
SDED nn	(nn+1) ← D (nn) ← E	LD (nn),DE	4	20
SHLD nn	(nn+1) ← H (nn) ← L	LD (nn),HL	3	16
SIXD nn	(nn+1) ← IX/H (nn) ← IX/L	LD (nn),IX	4	20
SIYD nn	(nn+1) ← IY/H (nn) ← IY/L	LD (nn),IY	4	20
SSPD nn	(nn+1) ← SP/H (nn) ← SP/L	LD (nn),SP	4	20
SPHL	SP ← HL	LD SP,HL	1	6
SPIX	SP ← IX	LD SP,IX	2	10
SPIY	SP ← IY	LD SP,IY	2	10
PUSH qq	(SP-1) ← qq/H (SP-2) ← qq/L SP ← SP-2	PUSH qq	1	11
PUSH ii	(SP-1) ← ii/H (SP-2) ← ii/L SP ← SP-2	PUSH ii	2	15
POP qq	qq/H ← (SP-1) qq/L ← (SP) SP ← SP-2	POP qq	1	10
POP ii	ii/H ← (SP+1) ii/L ← (SP) SP ← SP+2	POP ii	2	14

EXCHANGE, BLOCK TRANSFER, AND SEARCH GROUP

8080 MNEMONIC	OPERATION	ZILOG MNEMONIC	# OF BYTES	# OF T STATES
XCHC	HL ↔ DE	EX DE,HL	1	4
EXAF	PSW ↔ PSW'	EX AF,AF'	1	4
EXX	BCDEHL ↔ BCDEHL'	EXX	1	4

XTHL	H ↔(SP+1) L ↔(SP)	EX (SP),HL	1	19
XTIX	IX/H ↔(SP+1) IX/L ↔(SP)	EX (SP),IX	2	23
XTIY	IY/H ↔(SP+1) IY/L ↔(SP)	EX (SP),IY	2	23
LDI	(DE) ← (HL) DE ← DE+1 HL ← HL+1 BC ← BC-1	LDI	2	16
LDIR	repeat LDI until BC=∅	LDIR	2	21/16
LDD	(DE) ← (HL) DE ← DE-1 HL ← HL-1 BC ← BC-1	LDD	2	16
LDDR	repeat LDD until BC=∅	LDDR	2	21/16
CCI	A - (HL) HL ← HL+1 BC ← BC-1	CPI	2	16
CCIR	repeat CCI until A=(HL) or BC=∅	CPIR	2	21/16
CCD	A - (HL) HL ← HL-1 BC ← BC-1	CPD	2	16
CCDR	repeat CCD until A=(HL) or BC=∅	CPDR	2	21/16

8 BIT ARITHMETIC AND LOGICAL

8Ø8Ø MNEMONIC	OPERATION	ZILOG MNEMONIC	# OF BYTES	# OF T STATES
ADD r	A ← A + r	ADD A,r	1	4
ADD M	A ← A + (HL)	ADD A,(HL)	1	7
ADD d(ii)	A ← A + (ii+d)	ADD A,(Iii+d)	3	19
ADI n	A ← A + n	ADD A,n	2	7
ADC s	A ← A + s + CY	ADC A,s	As shown for ADD instruction	
ACI n	A ← A + n + CY	ADC A,n		
SUB s	A ← A - s	SUB s		

106

SUI n	$A \leftarrow A - n$	SUB n
SBB s	$A \leftarrow A - s - CY$	SBC A,s
SBI n	$A \leftarrow A - n - CY$	SBC A,n
ANA s	$A \leftarrow A \wedge s$	AND s
ANI n	$A \leftarrow A \wedge n$	AND n
ORA s	$A \leftarrow A \vee s$	OR s
ORI n	$A \leftarrow A \vee n$	OR n
XRA s	$A \leftarrow A \oplus s$	XOR s
XRI n	$A \leftarrow A \oplus n$	XOR n
CMP s	$A - s$	CP s
CPI n	$A - n$	CP n
INR r	$r \leftarrow r + 1$	INC r
INR M	$(HL) \leftarrow (HL) + 1$	INC (HL)
INR d(ii)	$(ii+d) \leftarrow (ii+d) + 1$	INC (Iii+d)
DCR r	$r \leftarrow r - 1$	DEC r
DCR M	$(HL) \leftarrow (HL) - 1$	DEC (HL)
DCR d(ii)	$(ii+d) \leftarrow (ii+d) - 1$	DEC (Iii+d)

GENERAL PURPOSE ARITHMETIC AND CONTROL GROUP

8Ø8Ø MNEMONIC	OPERATION	ZILOG MNEMONIC	# OF BYTES	# OF T STATES
DAA	convert A to packed BCD after an add or subtract of packed BCD operands	DAA	1	4
CMA	$A \leftarrow \sim A$	CPL	1	4
NEG	$A \leftarrow -A$	NEG	2	8
CMC	$CY \leftarrow \sim CY$	CCF	1	4
STC	$CY \leftarrow 1$	SCF	1	4
NOP	no operation	NOP	1	4
HLT	halt	HALT	1	4
DI	$IFF \leftarrow \emptyset$	DI	1	4
EI	$IFF \leftarrow 1$	EI	1	4

107

8Ø8Ø MNEMONIC	OPERATION	ZILOG MNEMONIC	# OF BYTES	# OF T STATES
IMØ	interrupt mode Ø	IM Ø	2	8
IM1	interrupt mode 1	IM 1	2	8
IM2	interrupt mode 2	IM 2	2	8

16 BIT ARITHMETIC GROUP

8Ø8Ø MNEMONIC	OPERATION	ZILOG MNEMONIC	# OF BYTES	# OF T STATES
DAD rr	HL ← HL + rr	ADD HL,rr	1	11
DADC rr	HL ← HL + rr + CY	ADC HL,rr	2	15
DSBC rr	HL ← HL − rr − CY	SBC HL,rr	2	15
DADX tt	IX ← IX + tt	ADD IX,tt	2	15
DADY uu	IY ← IY + uu	ADD IY,uu	2	15
INX rr	rr ← rr + 1	INC rr	1	6
INX ii	ii ← ii + 1	INC ii	2	1Ø
DCX rr	rr ← rr − 1	DEC rr	1	6
DCX ii	ii ← ii − 1	DEC ii	2	1Ø

ROTATE AND SHIFT GROUP

8Ø8Ø MNEMONIC	OPERATION	ZILOG MNEMONIC	# OF BYTES	# OF T STATES
RLC	CY ← [7 ← Ø] A	RLCA	1	4
RAL	CY ← [7 ← Ø] A	RLA	1	4
RRC	[7 → Ø] → CY A	RRCA	1	4
RAR	[7 → Ø] → CY A	RRA	1	4
RLCR r	Same diagram as for RLC	RLC r	2	8
RLCR M	"	RLC (HL)	2	15
RLCR d(ii)	"	RLC (Iii+d)	4	23

RALR s	Same diagram as for RAL	RL s	Same as for RLCR instruction
RRCR s	Same diagram as for RRC	RRC s	
RARR s	Same diagram as for RAR	RR s	

SLAR s $\boxed{CY} \leftarrow \boxed{7 \leftarrow \emptyset} \leftarrow \emptyset$ SLA s
              s

SRAR s $\boxed{7 \rightarrow \emptyset} \rightarrow \boxed{CY}$ SRA s
              s

SRLR s $\emptyset \rightarrow \boxed{7 \rightarrow \emptyset} \rightarrow \boxed{CY}$ SRL s
              s

RLD	A $\boxed{7\ \ 4\ 3\ \ \emptyset}$ (HL) $\boxed{7\ \ 4\ 3\ \ \emptyset}$	RLD	2	18
RRD	A $\boxed{7\ \ 4\ 3\ \ \emptyset}$ (HL) $\boxed{7\ \ 4\ 3\ \ \emptyset}$	RRD	2	18

BIT SET, RESET, AND TEST GROUP

8Ø8Ø MNEMONIC	OPERATION	ZILOG MNEMONIC	# OF BYTES	# OF T STATES
BIT b,r	ZF $\leftarrow \sim r\{b\}$	BIT b,r	2	8
BIT b,M	ZF $\leftarrow \sim(HL)\{b\}$	BIT b,(HL)	2	12
BIT b,d(ii)	ZF $\leftarrow \sim(Iii+d)\{b\}$	BIT b,(Iii+d)	4	2Ø
SET b,r	$r\{b\} \leftarrow 1$	SET b,r	2	8
SET b,m	$(HL)\{b\} \leftarrow 1$	SET b,(HL)	2	15
SET b,d(ii)	$(Iii+d)\{b\} \leftarrow 1$	SET b,(Iii+d)	4	23
RES b,s	$S\{b\} \leftarrow \emptyset$	RES b,s	Same as for SET instruction	

JUMP GROUP

8Ø8Ø MNEMONIC	OPERATION	ZILOG MNEMONIC	# OF BYTES	# OF T STATES
JMP nn	PC $\leftarrow$ nn	JP nn	3	1Ø
JZ nn	if zero, then JMP else continue	JP Z,nn	3	1Ø

8080 Mnemonic	Operation	Zilog Mnemonic	# of Bytes	# of T States
JNZ nn	if not zero	JP NZ,nn	3	10
JC nn	if carry	JP C,nn	3	10
JNC nn	if not carry	JP NC,nn	3	10
JPO nn	if parity odd	JP PO,nn	3	10
JPE nn	if parity even	JP PE,nn	3	10
JP nn	if sign positive	JP P,nn	3	10
JM nn	if sign negative	JP M,nn	3	10
JO nn	if overflow	JP PE,nn	3	10
JNO nn	if no overflow	JP PO,nn	3	10
JMPR nn	$PC \leftarrow PC + e$ where $e = nn - PC$ $-126 < e < 129$	JR e	2	12
JRZ nn	if zero, then JMPR else continue	JR Z,e	2	7/12
JRNZ nn	if not zero	JR NZ,e	2	7/12
JRC nn	if carry	JR C,e	2	7/12
JRNC nn	if not carry	JR NC,e	2	7/12
DJNZ nn	$B \leftarrow B - 1$ if B=0 then continue else JMPR	DJNZ e	2	8/13
PCHL	$PC \leftarrow HL$	JP (HL)	1	4
PCIX	$PC \leftarrow IX$	JP (IX)	2	8
PCIY	$PC \leftarrow IY$	JP (IY)	2	8

CALL AND RETURN GROUP

8080 Mnemonic	Operation	Zilog Mnemonic	# of Bytes	# of T States
CALL nn	$(SP-1) \leftarrow PC/H$ $(SP-2) \leftarrow PC/L$ $SP \leftarrow SP-2$ $PC \leftarrow nn$	CALL nn	3	17
CZ nn	if zero, then CALL else continue	CALL Z,nn	3	10/17
CNZ nn	if not zero	CALL NZ,nn	3	10/17
CC nn	if carry	CALL C,nn	3	10/17

CNC nn	if not carry	CALL NC,nn	3	1Ø/17
CPO nn	if parity odd	CALL PO,nn	3	1Ø/17
CPE nn	if parity even	CALL PE,nn	3	1Ø/17
CP nn	if sign positive	CALL P,nn	3	1Ø/17
CM nn	if sign negative	CALL M,nn	3	1Ø/17
CO nn	if overflow	CALL PE,nn	3	1Ø/17
CNO nn	if no overflow	CALL PO,nn	3	1Ø/17
RET	PC/H ← (SP+1) PC/L ← (SP) SP ← SP+2	RET	1	1Ø
RZ	if zero, then RET else continue	RET Z	1	5/11
RNZ	if not zero	RET NZ	1	5/11
RC	if carry	RET C	1	5/11
RNC	if not carry	RET NC	1	5/11
RPO	if parity odd	RET PO	1	5/11
RPE	if parity even	RET PE	1	5/11
RP	if sign positive	RET P	1	5/11
RM	if sign negative	RET M	1	5/11
RO	if overflow	RET PE	1	5/11
RNO	if no overflow	RET PO	1	5/11
RETI	return from interrupt	RETI	2	14
RETN	return from non- maskable interrupt	RETN	2	14
RST n	(SP-1) ← PC/H (SP-2) ← PC/L PC ← 8 * n where $0 \leq n < 8$	RST n	1	11

INPUT AND OUTPUT GROUP

8Ø8Ø MNEMONIC	OPERATION	ZILOG MNEMONIC	# OF BYTES	# OF T STATES
IN n	A ← In	IN A,(n)	2	11
INP r	r ← I(C)	IN r,(C)	2	12

111

INI	(HL) ← I(C) B ← B - 1 HL ← HL + 1	INI	2	16
INIR	repeat INI until B=∅	INIR	2	16/21
IND	(HL) ← I(C) B ← B - 1 HL ← HL - 1	IND	2	16
INDR	repeat IND until B=∅	INDR	2	16/21
OUT n	On ← A	OUT (n),A	2	11
OUTP r	O(C) ← r	OUT (C),r	2	12
OUTI	O(C) ← (HL) B ← B - 1 HL ← HL + 1	OUTI	2	16
OUTIR	repeat OUTI until B=∅	OTIR	2	16/21
OUTD	O(C) ← (HL) B ← B - 1 HL ← HL - 1	OUTD	2	16
OUTDR	repeat OUTD until B=∅	OTDR	2	16/21

APPENDIX B
ASCII CHARACTER SET

ØØ Ctrl-@ (NUL)	2Ø space	4Ø @	6Ø `
Ø1 Ctrl-A (SOH)	21 !	41 A	61 a
Ø2 Ctrl-B (STX)	22 "	42 B	62 b
Ø3 Ctrl-C (ETX)	23 #	43 C	63 c
Ø4 Ctrl-D (EOT)	24 $	44 D	64 d
Ø5 Ctrl-E (ENQ)	25 %	45 E	65 e
Ø6 Ctrl-F (ACK)	26 &	46 F	66 f
Ø7 Ctrl-G (BEL)	27 '	47 G	67 g
Ø8 Ctrl-H (BS)	28 (	48 H	68 h
Ø9 Ctrl-I (HT)	29)	49 I	69 i
ØA Ctrl-J (LF)	2A *	4A J	6A j
ØB Ctrl-K (VT)	2B +	4B K	6B k
ØC Ctrl-L (FF)	2C ,	4C L	6C l
ØD Ctrl-M (CR)	2D -	4D M	6D m
ØE Ctrl-N (SO)	2E .	4E N	6E n
ØF Ctrl-O (SI)	2F /	4F O	6F o
1Ø Ctrl-P (DLE)	3Ø Ø	5Ø P	7Ø p
11 Ctrl-Q (DC1)	31 1	51 Q	7] q
12 Ctrl-R (DC2)	32 2	52 R	72 r
13 Ctrl-S (DC3)	33 3	53 S	73 s
14 Ctrl-T (DC4)	34 4	54 T	74 t
15 Ctrl-U (NAK)	35 5	55 U	75 u
16 Ctrl-V (SYN)	36 6	56 V	76 v
17 Ctrl-W (ETB)	37 7	57 W	77 w
18 Ctrl-X (CAN)	38 8	58 X	78 x
19 Ctrl-Y (EM)	39 9	59 Y	79 y
1A Ctrl-Z (SUB)	3A :	5A Z	7A z
1B Ctrl-[(ESC)	3B ;	5B [	7B {
1C Ctrl-\ (FS)	3C <	5C \	7C	
1D Ctrl-] (GS)	3D =	5D]	7D }
1E Ctrl-^ (RS)	3E >	5E ^	7E ~
1F Ctrl-- (US)	3F ?	5F _	7F DEL

APPENDIX C

8Ø8Ø Disassembler

(Including Single Byte Z-8Ø Instructions)

HEX	EXTENDED OP CODE	MNEMONIC	HEX	EXTENDED OP CODE	MNEMONIC
ØØ		NOP	1B		DCX D
Ø1	nn	LXI B,nn	1C		INR E
Ø2		STAX B	1D		DCR D
Ø3		INX B	1E	N	MVI E,n
Ø4		INR B	1F		RAR
Ø5		DCR B	2Ø	e^{-2}	JRNZ nn
Ø6	n	MVI B,n	21	nn	LXI H,nn
Ø7		RLC	22	nn	SHLD nn
Ø8		EXAF	23		INX H
Ø9		DAD B	24		INR H
ØA		LDAX B	25		DCR H
ØB		DCX B	26	n	MVI H,n
ØC		INR C	27		DAA
ØD		DCR C	28	e^{-2}	JRZ nn
ØE	N	MVI C,n	29		DAD H
ØF		RRC	2A	nn	LHLD nn
1Ø	e^{-2}	DJNZ nn	2B		DCX H
11	nn	LXI D,nn	2C		INR L
12		STAX D	2D		DCR L
13		INX D	2E	n	MVI L,n
14		INR D	2F		CMA
15		DCR D	3Ø	e^{-2}	JRNC nn
16	n	MVI D,n	31	nn	LXI SP,nn
17		RAL	32	nn	STA nn
18	e^{-2}	JMPR nn	33		INX SP
19		DAD D	34		INR M
1A		LDAX D	35		DCR M

114

HEX	EXTENDED OP CODE	MNEMONIC	HEX	EXTENDED OP CODE	MNEMONIC
36	n	MVI M,n	54		MOV D,H
37		STC	55		MOV D,L
38	e^{-2}	JRC nn	56		MOV D,M
39		DAD SP	57		MOV D,A
3A	nn	LDA nn	58		MOV E,B
3B		DCX SP	59		MOV E,C
3C		INR A	5A		MOV E,D
3D		DCR A	5B		MOV E,E
3E	n	MVI A,n	5C		MOV E,H
3F		CMC	5D		MOV E,L
4∅		MOV B,B	5E		MOV E,M
41		MOV B,C	5F		MOV E,A
42		MOV B,D	6∅		MOV H,B
43		MOV B,E	61		MOV H,C
44		MOV B,H	62		MOV H,D
45		MOV B,L	63		MOVH,E
46		MOV B,M	64		MOV H,H
47		MOV B,A	65		MOV H,L
48		MOV C,B	66		MOV H,M
49		MOV C,C	67		MOV H,A
4A		MOV C,D	68		MOV L,B
4B		MOV C,E	69		MOV L,C
4C		MOV C,H	6A		MOV L,D
4D		MOV C,L	6B		MOV L,E
4E		MOV C,M	6C		MOV L,H
4F		MOV C,A	6D		MOV L,L
5∅		MOV D,B	6E		MOV L,M
51		MOV D,C	6F		MOV L,A
52		MOV D,D	7∅		MOV M,B
53		MOV D,E	71		MOV M,C

115

HEX	EXTENDED OP CODE	MNEMONIC	HEX	EXTENDED OP CODE	MNEMONIC
72		MOV M,D	9∅		SUB B
73		MOV M,E	91		SUB C
74		MOV M,H	92		SUB D
75		MOV M,L	93		SUB E
76		HLT	94		SUB H
77		MOV M,A	95		SUB L
78		MOV A,B	96		SUB M
79		MOV A,C	97		SUB A
7A		MOV A,D	98		SBB B
7B		MOV A,E	99		SBB C
7C		MOV A,H	9A		SBB D
7D		MOV A,L	9B		SBB E
7E		MOV A,M	9C		SBB H
7F		MOV A,A	9D		SBB L
8∅		ADD B	9E		SBB M
81		ADD C	9F		SBB A
82		ADD D	A∅		ANA B
83		ADD E	A1		ANA C
84		ADD H	A2		ANA D
85		ADD L	A3		ANA E
86		ADD M	A4		ANA H
87		ADD A	A5		ANA L
88		ADC B	A6		ANA M
89		ADC C	A7		ANA A
8A		ADC D	A8		XRA B
8B		ADC E	A9		XRA C
8C		ADC H	AA		XRA D
8D		ADC L	AB		XRA D
8E		ADC M	AB		XRA E
8F		ADC A	AC		XRA H

HEX	EXTENDED OP CODE	MNEMONIC	HEX	EXTENDED OP CODE	MNEMONIC
AD		XRA L	CC	nn	CZ nn
AE		XRA M	CD	nn	CALL nn
AF		XRA A	CE	n	ACI n
BØ		ORA B	CF		RST 1
B1		ORA C	DØ		RNC
B2		ORA D	D1		POP D
B3		ORA E	D2	nn	JNC nn
B4		ORA H	D3	n	OUT n
B5		ORA L	D4	nn	CNC nn
B6		ORA M	D5		PUSH D
B7		ORA A	D6	n	SUI n
B8		CMP B	D7		RST 2
B9		CMP C	D8		RC
BA		CMP D	D9		EXX
BB		CMP E	DA	nn	JC nn
BC		CMP H	DB		LDAX B
BD		CMP L	DC	nn	CC nn
BE		CMP M	DE	n	SBB n
BF		CMP A	DF		RST 3
CØ		RNZ	EØ		RPO
C1		POP B	E1		POP H
C2	nn	JNZ NN	E2	nn	JPO nn
C3	nn	JMP nn	E3		XTHL
C4	nn	CNZ nn	E4	nn	CPO nn
C5		PUSH B	E5		PUSH H
C6	n	ADI n	E6	n	ANI n
C7		RST Ø	E7		RST 4
C8		RZ	E8		RPE
C9		RET	E9		PCHL
CA	nn	JZ nn	EA	nn	JPE nn

HEX	EXTENDED OP CODE	MNEMONIC	HEX	EXTENDED OP CODE	MNEMONIC
EB		XCHG	F6	n	ORI n
EC	nn	CPE nn	F7		RST 6
EE	n	XRI n	F8		RM
EF		RST 5	F9		SPHL
FØ		RP	FA	nn	JM nn
F1		POP PSW	FB		EI
F2	nn	JP nn	FC	nn	CM nn
F3		DI	FE	n	CPI n
F4	nn	CP nn	FF		RST 7
F5		PUSH PSW			

Z-8Ø Extension Disassembler

HEX	EXTENDED OP CODE	MNEMONIC	HEX	EXTENDED OP CODE	MNEMONIC
CB	ØØ	RLC B	CB	1C	RR H
CB	Ø1	RLC C	CB	1D	RR L
CB	Ø2	RLC D	CB	1E	RR (HL)
CB	Ø3	RLC E	CB	1F	RR A
CB	Ø4	RLC H	CB	2Ø	SLA B
CB	Ø5	RLC L	CB	21	SLA C
CB	Ø6	RLC (HL)	CB	22	SLA D
CB	Ø7	RLC A	CB	23	SLA E
CB	Ø8	RRC B	CB	24	SLA H
CB	Ø9	RRC C	CB	25	SLA L
CB	ØA	RRC D	CB	26	SLA (HL)
CB	ØB	RRC E	CB	27	SLA A
CB	ØC	RRC H	CB	28	SRA B
CB	ØD	RRC L	CB	29	SRA C
CB	ØE	RRC (HL)	CB	2A	SRA D
CB	ØF	RRC A	CB	2B	SRA E
CB	1Ø	RL B	CB	2C	SRA H
CB	11	RL C	CB	2D	SRA L
CD	12	RL D	CB	2E	SRA (HL)
CB	13	RL E	CB	2F	SRA A
CB	14	RL H	CB	38	SRL B
CB	15	RL L	CB	39	SRL C
CB	16	RL (HL)	CB	3A	SRL D
CB	17	RL A	CB	3B	SRL E
CB	18	RR B	CB	3C	SRL H
CB	19	RR C	CB	3D	SRL L
CB	1A	RR D	CB	3E	SRL (HL)
CB	1B	RR E	CB	3F	SRL A

119

HEX	EXTENDED OP CODE	MNEMONIC	HEX	EXTENDED OP CODE	MNEMONIC
CB	4Ø	BIT Ø,B	CB	5E	BIT 3,(HL)
CB	41	BIT Ø,C	CB	5F	BIT 3,A
CB	42	BIT Ø,D	CB	6Ø	BIT 4,B
CB	43	BIT Ø,E	CB	61	BIT 4,C
CB	44	BIT Ø,H	CB	62	BIT 4,D
CB	45	BIT Ø,L	CB	63	BIT 4,E
CB	46	BIT Ø,(HL)	CB	64	BIT 4,H
CB	47	BIT Ø,A	CB	65	BIT 4,L
CB	48	BIT 1,B	CB	66	BIT 4,(HL)
CB	49	BIT 1,C	CB	67	BIT 4,A
CB	4A	BIT 1,D	CB	68	BIT 5,B
CB	4B	BIT 1,E	CB	69	BIT 5,C
CB	4C	BIT 1,H	CB	6A	BIT 5,D
CB	4D	BIT 1,L	CB	6B	BIT 5,E
CB	4E	BIT 1,(HL)	CB	6C	BIT 5,H
CB	4F	BIT 1,A	CB	6D	BIT 5,L
CB	5Ø	BIT 2,B	CB	6E	BIT 5,(HL)
CB	51	BIT 2,C	CB	6F	BIT 5,A
CB	52	BIT 2,D	CB	7Ø	BIT 6,B
CB	53	BIT 2,E	CB	71	BIT 6,C
CB	54	BIT 2,H	CB	72	BIT 6,D
CB	55	BIT 2,L	CB	73	BIT 6,E
CB	56	BIT 2,(HL)	CB	74	BIT 6,H
CB	57	BIT 2,A	GB	75	BIT 6,L
CB	58	BIT 3,B	CB	76	BIT 6,(HL)
CB	59	BIT 3,C	CB	77	BIT 6,A
CB	5A	BIT 3,D	CB	78	BIT 7,B
CB	5B	BIT 3,E	CB	79	BIT 7,C
CB	5C	BIT 3,H	CB	7A	BIT 7,D
CB	5D	BIT 3,L	CB	7B	BIT 7,E

HEX	EXTENDED OP CODE	MNEMONIC	HEX	EXTENDED OP CODE	MNEMONIC
CB	7C	BIT 7,H	CB	9A	RES 3,D
CB	7D	BIT 7,L	CB	9B	RES 3,E
CB	7E	BIT 7,(HL)	CB	9C	RES 3,H
CB	7F	BIT 7,A	CB	9D	RES 3,L
CB	8Ø	RES Ø,B	CB	9E	RES 3,(HL)
CB	81	RES Ø,C	CB	9F	RES 3,A
CB	82	RES Ø,D	CB	AØ	RES 4,B
CB	83	RES Ø,E	CB	A1	RES 4,C
CB	84	RES Ø,H	CB	A2	RES 4,D
CB	85	RES Ø,L	CB	A3	RES 4,E
CB	86	RES Ø,(HL)	CB	A4	RES 4,H
CB	87	RES Ø,A	CB	A5	RES 4,L
CB	88	RES 1,B	CB	A6	RES 4,(HL)
CB	89	RES 1,C	CB	A7	RES 4,A
CB	8A	RES 1,D	CB	A8	RES 5,B
CB	8B	RES 1,E	CB	A9	RES 5,C
CB	8C	RES 1,H	CB	AA	RES 5,D
CB	8D	RES 1,L	CB	AB	RES 5,E
CB	8E	RES 1,(HL)	CB	AC	RES 5,H
CB	8F	RES 1,A	CB	AD	RES 5,L
CB	9Ø	RES 2,B	CB	AE	RES 5,(HL)
CB	91	RES 2,C	CB	AF	RES 5,A
CB	92	RES 2,D	CB	BØ	RES 6,B
CB	93	RES 2,E	CB	B1	RES 6,C
CB	94	RES 2,H	CB	B2	RES 6,D
CB	95	RES 2,L	CB	B3	RES 6,E
CB	96	RES 2,(HL)	CB	B4	RES 6,H
CB	97	RES 2,A	CB	B5	RES 6,L
CB	98	RES 3,B	CB	B6	RES 6,(HL)
CB	99	RES 3,C	CB	B7	RES 6,A

121

HEX	EXTENDED OP CODE	MNEMONIC	HEX	EXTENDED OP CODE	MNEMONIC
CB	B8	RES 7,B	CB	D6	SET 2,(HL)
CB	B9	RES 7,C	CB	D7	SET 2,A
CB	BA	RES 7,D	CB	D8	SET 3,B
CB	BB	RES 7,E	CB	D9	SET 3,C
CB	BC	RES 7,H	CB	DA	SET 3,D
CB	BD	RES 7,L	CB	DB	SET 3,E
CB	BE	RES 7,(HL)	CB	DC	SET 3,H
CB	BF	RES 7,A	CB	DD	SET 3,L
CB	CØ	SET Ø,B	CB	DE	SET 3,(HL)
CB	C1	SET Ø,C	CB	DF	SET 3,A
CB	C2	SET Ø,D	CB	EØ	SET 4,B
CB	C3	SET Ø,E	CB	E1	SET 4,C
CB	C4	SET Ø,H	CB	E2	SET 4,D
CB	C5	SET Ø,L	CB	E3	SET 4,E
CB	C6	SET Ø,(HL)	CB	E4	SET 4,H
CB	C7	SET Ø,A	CB	E5	SET 4,L
CB	C8	SET 1,B	CB	E6	SET 4,(HL)
CB	C9	SET 1,C	CB	E7	SET 4,A
CB	CA	SET 1,D	CB	E8	SET 5,B
CB	CB	SET 1,E	CB	E9	SET 5,C
CB	CC	SET 1,H	CB	EA	SET 5,D
CB	CD	SET 1,L	CB	EB	SET 5,E
CB	CE	SET 1,(HL)	CB	EC	SET 5,H
CB	CF	SET 1,A	CB	ED	SET 5,L
CB	DØ	SET 2,B	CB	EE	SET 5,(HL)
CB	D1	SET 2,C	CB	EF	SET 5,A
CB	D2	SET 2,D	CB	FØ	SET 6,B
CB	D3	SET 2,E	CB	F1	SET 6,C
CB	D4	SET 2,H	CB	F2	SET 6,D
CB	D5	SET 2,L	CB	F3	SET 6,E

HEX	EXTENDED OP CODE	MNEMONIC	HEX	EXTENDED OP CODE	MNEMONIC
CB	F4	SET 6,H	DD	70 d	LD (IX+d),B
CB	F5	SET 6,L	DD	71 d	LD (IX+d),C
CB	F6	SET 6,(HL)	DD	72 d	LD (IX+d),D
CB	F7	SET 6,A	DD	73 d	LD (IX+d),E
CB	F8	SET 7,B	DD	74 d	LD (IX+d),H
CB	F9	SET 7,C	DD	75 d	LD (IX+d),L
CB	FA	SET 7,D	DD	77 d	LD (IX+d),A
CB	FB	SET 7,E	DD	7E d	LD A,(IX+d)
CB	FC	SET 7,H	DD	86 d	ADD A,(IX+d)
CB	FD	SET 7,L	DD	8E d	ADC A,(IX+d)
CB	FE	SET 7,(HL)	DD	96 d	SUB (IX+d)
CB	FF	SET 7,A	DD	9E d	SBC A,(IX+d)
DD	09	DAD IX,BC	DD	A6 d	AND (IX+d)
DD	19	DAD IX,DE	DD	AE d	XOR (IX+d)
DD	21 nn	LD IX,nn	DD	B6 d	OR (IX+d)
DD	22 nn	LD (nn),IX	DD	BE d	CP (IX+d)
DD	23	INC IX	DD	CB d 06	RLC (IX+d)
DD	29	DAD IX,IX	DD	CB d 0E	RRC (IX+d)
DD	2A nn	LD IX,(nn)	DD	CB d 16	RL (IX+d)
DD	2B	DEC IX	DD	CB d 1E	RR (IX+d)
DD	34 d	INC (IX+d)	DD	CB d 26	SLA (IX+d)
DD	35 d	DEC (IX+d)	DD	CB d 2E	SRA (IX+d)
DD	36 d n	LD (IX+d),n	DD	CB d 3E	SRLR (IX+d)
DD	39	DAD IX,SP	DD	CB d 46	BIT 0,(IX+d)
DD	46 d	LD B,(IX+d)	DD	CB d 4E	BIT 1,(IX+d)
DD	4E d	LD C,(IX+d)	DD	CB d 56	BIT 2,(IX+d)
DD	56 d	LD D,(IX+d)	DD	CB d 5E	BIT 3,(IX+d)
DD	5E d	LD E,(IX+d)	DD	CB d 66	BIT 4,(IX+d)
DD	66 d	LD H,(IX+d)	DD	CB d 6E	BIT 5,(IX+d)
DD	6E d	LD L,(IX+d)	DD	CB d 76	BIT 6,(IX+d)

HEX	EXTENDED OP CODE	MNEMONIC	HEX	EXTENDED OP CODE	MNEMONIC
DD	CB d 7E	BIT 7,(IX+d)	ED	4D	RETI
DD	CB d 86	RES Ø,(IX+d)	ED	4F	LD R,A
DD	CB d 8E	RES 1,(IX+d)	ED	52	SBC DE
DD	CB d 96	RES 2,(IX+d)	ED	53 nn	LD (nn),DE
DD	CB d 9E	RES 3,(IX+d)	ED	57	LD A,I
DD	CB d A6	RES 4,(IX+d)	ED	5A	ADC HL,DE
DD	CB d AE	RES 5,(IX+d)	ED	5B nn	LD DE,(nn)
DD	CB d B6	RES 6,(IX+d)	ED	5F	LD A,R
DD	CB d BE	RES 7,(IX+d)	ED	62	SBC HL,HL
DD	CB d C6	SET Ø,(IX+d)	ED	67	RRD
DD	CB d CE	SET 1,(IX+d)	ED	6A	ADC HL,HL
DD	CB d D6	SET 2,(IX+d)	ED	6F	RLD
DD	CB d DE	SET 3,(IX+d)	ED	72	SBC HL,SP
DD	CB d E6	SET 4,(IX+d)	ED	73 nn	LD (nn),SP
DD	CB d EE	SET 5,(IX+d)	ED	7A	ADC HL,SP
DD	CB d F6	SET 6,(IX+d)	ED	7B	LD SP,(nn)
DD	CB d FE	SET 7,(IX+d)	ED	AØ	LDI
DD	E1	POP IX	ED	A1	CPI
DD	E3	EX (SP),IX	ED	A8	LDD
DD	E5	PUSH IX	ED	A9	CPD
DD	E9	JP (IX)	ED	BØ	LDIR
DD	F9	LD SP,IX	ED	B1	CPIR
ED	42	SBC HL,BC	ED	B8	LDDR
ED	43 nn	LD (nn),BC	ED	B9	CPDR
ED	44	NEG			
ED	45	RETN	FD	See DD instruction.	
ED	47	LD I,A		Substitute "Y" for every	
ED	4A	ADC HL,BC		"X" - e.g. ADD IX,IX	
ED	4B nn	LD BC,(nn)		becomes ADD IY,IY	

1a) 101 =

$$1 \times 2^0 = 1$$
$$+ 0 \times 2^1 \quad 0$$
$$+ 1 \times 2^2 \quad \underline{+ 4}$$
$$5$$

b) 1101 =

$$1 \times 2^0 = 1$$
$$+ 0 \times 2^1 \quad 0$$
$$+ 1 \times 2^2 \quad 4$$
$$+ 1 \times 2^3 \quad \underline{+ 8}$$
$$13$$

c) 11101 =

$$1 \times 2^0 = 1$$
$$+ 0 \times 2^1 \quad 0$$
$$+ 1 \times 2^2 \quad 4$$
$$+ 1 \times 2^3 \quad 8$$
$$+ 1 \times 2^4 \quad \underline{+ 16}$$
$$29$$

d) 101011 =

$$1 \times 2^0 = 1$$
$$+ 1 \times 2^1 \quad 2$$
$$+ 0 \times 2^2 \quad 0$$
$$+ 1 \times 2^3 \quad 8$$
$$+ 0 \times 2^4 \quad 0$$
$$+ 1 \times 2^5 \quad \underline{+ 32}$$
$$43$$

e) 10000000 =

$$0 \times 2^0 = 0$$
$$+ 0 \times 2^1 \quad 0$$
$$+ 0 \times 2^2 \quad 0$$
$$+ 0 \times 2^3 \quad 0$$
$$+ 0 \times 2^4 \quad 0$$
$$+ 0 \times 2^5 \quad 0$$
$$+ 0 \times 2^6 \quad 0$$
$$+ 1 \times 2^7 \quad \underline{+128}$$
$$128$$

f) 11001010 =

$$0 \times 2^0 = 0$$
$$+ 1 \times 2^1 \quad 2$$
$$+ 0 \times 2^2 \quad 0$$
$$+ 1 \times 2^3 \quad 8$$
$$+ 0 \times 2^4 \quad 0$$
$$+ 0 \times 2^5 \quad 0$$
$$+ 1 \times 2^6 \quad 64$$
$$+ 1 \times 2^7 \quad \underline{+128}$$
$$202$$

g) 10001110 =

$$0 \times 2^0 = 0$$
$$+ 1 \times 2^1 \quad 2$$
$$+ 1 \times 2^2 \quad 4$$
$$+ 1 \times 2^3 \quad 8$$
$$+ 0 \times 2^4 \quad 0$$
$$+ 0 \times 2^5 \quad 0$$
$$+ 0 \times 2^6 \quad 0$$
$$+ 1 \times 2^7 \quad \underline{+128}$$
$$142$$

h) 11111001 =

$$1 \times 2^0 = 1$$
$$+ 0 \times 2^1 \quad 0$$
$$+ 0 \times 2^2 \quad 0$$
$$+ 1 \times 2^3 \quad 8$$
$$+ 1 \times 2^4 \quad 16$$
$$+ 1 \times 2^5 \quad 32$$
$$+ 1 \times 2^6 \quad 64$$
$$+ 1 \times 2^7 \quad \underline{+128}$$
$$\cdot \ 249$$

i) 00010010

$= 0 \times 2^0 = 0$
$+ 1 \times 2^1 \quad 2$
$+ 0 \times 2^2 \quad 0$
$+ 0 \times 2^3 \quad 0$
$+ 1 \times 2^4 \quad 16$
$+ 0 \times 2^5 \quad 0$
$+ 0 \times 2^6 \quad 0$
$+ 0 \times 2^7 \quad \underline{+ 0}$
$\qquad\qquad 18$

k) 111000100

$= 0 \times 2^0 = 0$
$+ 0 \times 2^1 \quad 0$
$+ 1 \times 2^2 \quad 4$
$+ 0 \times 2^3 \quad 0$
$+ 0 \times 2^4 \quad 0$
$+ 0 \times 2^5 \quad 0$
$+ 1 \times 2^6 \quad 64$
$+ 1 \times 2^7 \quad 128$
$+ 1 \times 2^8 \quad \underline{+256}$
$\qquad\qquad 452$

l) 1010101011

$= 1 \times 2^0 = 1$
$+ 1 \times 2^1 \quad 2$
$+ 0 \times 2^2 \quad 0$
$+ 1 \times 2^3 \quad 8$
$+ 0 \times 2^4 \quad 0$
$+ 1 \times 2^5 \quad 32$
$+ 0 \times 2^6 \quad 0$
$+ 1 \times 2^7 \quad 128$
$+ 0 \times 2^8 \quad 0$
$+ 1 \times 2^9 \quad \underline{+512}$
$\qquad\qquad 683$

j) 01110011

$= 1 \times 2^0 = 1$
$+ 1 \times 2^1 \quad 2$
$+ 0 \times 2^2 \quad 0$
$+ 0 \times 2^3 \quad 0$
$+ 1 \times 2^4 \quad 16$
$+ 1 \times 2^5 \quad 32$
$+ 1 \times 2^6 \quad 64$
$+ 0 \times 2^7 \quad \underline{+ 0}$
$\qquad\qquad 115$

2a) $6_D = 6_H = 0110_B$

b) $14_D = E_H = 1110_B$

c) $127_D = \begin{array}{r} 7 \text{ r } 15 \\ 16\,\overline{)127} \end{array} = 7F_H = 01111111_B$

d) $280_D = \begin{array}{r} 1 \text{ r } 24 \\ 256\,\overline{)280} \end{array} = 118_H = 000100011000_B$

e) $542_D = \begin{array}{r} 2 \text{ r } 30 \\ 256\,\overline{)542} \end{array} = 21E_H = 001000011110_B$

$\begin{array}{r} 1 \text{ r } 14 \\ 16\,\overline{)30} \end{array}$

f) $1077_D = \begin{array}{r} 4 \text{ r } 53 \\ 256\,\overline{)1077} \end{array} = 435_H = 010000110101_B$

$\begin{array}{r} 3 \text{ r } 5 \\ 16\,\overline{)53} \end{array}$

126

g) 4095_D = $\dfrac{15\ r\ 255}{256\,\overline{)4095}}$ = FFF_H = 111111111111_B

$\dfrac{15\ r\ 15}{16\,\overline{)255}}$

h) 8702_D = $\dfrac{2\ r\ 510}{4096\,\overline{)8702}}$ = $21FE_H$

$\dfrac{1\ r\ 254}{256\,\overline{)510}}$ = 0010000111111110_B

$\dfrac{15\ r\ 14}{16\,\overline{)254}}$

i) $15,430_D$ = $\dfrac{3\ r\ 3142}{4096\,\overline{)15430}}$ = $3C46_H$

$\dfrac{12\ r\ 70}{256\,\overline{)3142}}$ = 0011110001000110

$\dfrac{4\ r\ 6}{16\,\overline{)70}}$

j) $43,751_D$ = $\dfrac{10\ r\ 2791}{4096\,\overline{43751}}$ = $AAE7_H$

$\dfrac{10\ r\ 231}{256\,\overline{2791}}$ = 1010101011100111_B

$\dfrac{14\ r\ 7}{16\,\overline{231}}$

k) $65,552_D$ = $\dfrac{1\ r\ 16}{65536\,\overline{65552}}$ = 10010_H

$\dfrac{0\ r\ 16}{4096\,\overline{16}}$ = 0001000000000000010000_B

$\dfrac{0\ r\ 16}{256\,\overline{16}}$

$\dfrac{1\ r\ 0}{16\,\overline{16}}$

1) $70,980_D = $ $\dfrac{1}{65536\ \overline{70980}}$ r 5444 = 11544_H

             $\dfrac{1}{4096\ \overline{5444}}$ r 1348 = $0001000101010100010 0_B$

             $\dfrac{5}{256\ \overline{1348}}$ r 68

             $\dfrac{4}{16\ \overline{68}}$ r 4

3a) 00000111 = 7   11111000
                        + 1
                  11111001 = −7

b) 00010001 = 17   11101110
                        + 1
                  11101111 = −17

c) 00010111 = 23   11101000
                        + 1
                  11101001 = −23

d) 00110000 = 48   11001111
                        + 1
                  11010000 = −48

e) 01101000 = 104   10010111
                        + 1
                  10011000 = −104

f) 01111111 = 127   10000000
                        + 1
                  10000001 = −127

4a) 00001001 = 9

b) ØØØ11ØØ1 = 25

c) 1111IØ11   ØØØØØ1ØØ
                         + 1
                   ØØØØØ1Ø1 = 5, so 11111Ø11 = -5

d) ØØ1ØØ111 = 27$_H$ = 39

e) 1111ØØ1Ø   ØØØØ11Ø1
                         + 1
                   ØØØØ111Ø = 14, so 1111ØØ1Ø = -14

f) 11Ø1ØØØØ   ØØ1Ø1111
                         + 1
                   ØØ11ØØØØ = 3Ø$_H$ = 48, so 11Ø1ØØØØ = -48

5a) ØØØØ1Ø11   =   11   No Carry
    + ØØØØ1111   + 15   No Overflow
     ØØØ11Ø1Ø   26

b) ØØØ1ØØØ1   =   17   No Carry
   + 111Ø1Ø11   +(-21)   No Overflow
    1111111ØØ   -4

c) ØØ1Ø111Ø   =   46   No Carry
   - ØØØØ11ØØ   - 12   No Overflow
    ØØ1ØØØ1Ø   34

d) Ø11Ø1ØØØ   ≠   1Ø4   No Carry
   + ØØ11Ø111   + 55   Overflow
    1ØØ11111   159

129

e) 10111101 ≠ – 67   No Carry
   – 01101011   –107   Overflow
    01010010   –174

f) 10111101   – 67   Carry
   + 01101011   +107   No Overflow
  1 00101000   40

6a) | AND | OR | XOR |
|---|---|---|
| 00000000 | 11010101 | 11010101 |
| Carry= 0 | C= 0 | C= 0 |
| Zero = 1 | Z= 0 | Z= 0 |
| Sign = 0 | S= 1 | S= 1 |
| Parity=1 | P= 0 | P= 0 |

b) | 10110100 | 11111111 | 01001011 |
|---|---|---|
| C= 0 | C= 0 | C= 0 |
| Z= 0 | Z= 0 | Z= 0 |
| S= 1 | S= 1 | S= 0 |
| P= 1 | P= 1 | P= 1 |

c) | AND | OR | XOR |
|---|---|---|
| 00010110 | 11111111 | 11101001 |
| C= 0 | C= 0 | C= 0 |
| Z= 0 | Z= 0 | Z= 0 |
| S= 0 | S= 1 | S= 1 |
| P= 0 | P= 1 | P= 0 |

d) | 10100010 | 11110111 | 01010101 |
|---|---|---|
| C= 0 | C= 0 | C= 0 |
| Z= 0 | Z= 0 | Z= 0 |
| S= 1 | S= 1 | S= 0 |
| P= 0 | P= 0 | P= 1 |

e) | 00010000 | 10011101 | 10001101 |
|---|---|---|
| C= 0 | C= 0 | C= 0 |
| Z= 0 | Z= 0 | Z= 0 |
| S= 0 | S= 1 | S= 1 |
| P= 0 | P= 0 | P= 1 |

f)　　00000000　　　11110001　　　11110001
　　　　C= 0　　　　　C= 0　　　　　C= 0
　　　　Z= 1　　　　　Z= 0　　　　　Z= 0
　　　　S= 0　　　　　S= 1　　　　　S= 1
　　　　P= 1　　　　　P= 0　　　　　P= 0

g)　　00000000　　　11111111　　　11111111
　　　　C= 0　　　　　C= 0　　　　　C= 0
　　　　Z= 1　　　　　Z= 0　　　　　Z= 0
　　　　S= 0　　　　　S= 1　　　　　S= 1
　　　　P= 1　　　　　P= 1　　　　　P= 1

h)　　11001111　　　11001111　　　00000000
　　　　C= 0　　　　　C= 0　　　　　C= 0
　　　　Z= 0　　　　　Z= 0　　　　　Z= 1
　　　　S= 1　　　　　S= 1　　　　　S= 0
　　　　P= 1　　　　　P= 1　　　　　P= 1

WHERE IS MY VARIABLE?

1)	8080	Z-80	the point is that an
	MOV A,D	LD A,D	intermediate storage
	MOV D,E	LD D,E	area must be used
	MOV E,A	LD F,A	

2) 11110100

3) After the first instruction HL contains:
　　2039, so HL now points to a new location.

　　After the second instruction A contains:
　　00

4) 3AF334

5) Interprets the contents of index register IX as an address. Takes that address plus 12 and loads the contents of the byte into register E.

6) The first loads the value of the two bytes beginning at SPOT into register pair HL. The second loads the address of SPOT into register pair HL.

7) AF 4020$_H$.   The registers are swapped.

8) No.

9) a)   LXI   SP,6F32H   (8080)   NOTE: Assemblers differ on the form

   LD   SP,6F32H   (Z-80)   Hex numbers must be written in. The

   assembler will put it in swapped format

   within the instruction.

9)   b)   BC = 0302

   SP = 6F34

10)   Here is a blow-by-blow account of the effects:

   a)   Register A contains the value 3.

   b)   Memory location 2400 contains the value 3.

   c)   Index register IX contains, after unswapping, 2403$_H$.

   d)   Register C contains the value 21.

A METHOD TO OUR LOGIC

1)   8080   Z-80
   SUB   A   SUB   A
   ADD   M   ADD   A,(HL)
   INX   H   INC   HL
   ADD   M   ADD   A
   INX   H   INC   HL
   ADD   M   ADD   A,(HL)

2)
```
MOV  A,C          LF   A,C
ADD  L            ADD  A,L
MOV  L,A          LD   L,A
MOV  A,B          LD   A,B
ADC  H            ADC  A,H
MOV  H,A          LD   H,A
```

3) Desired bit pattern: 11111010 = FA_H

   CPI FAH   CP   FAH

   The zero flag will be set on a match.

4) Signed V XORS = 1
   Unsigned C = 1

5) a) Load into the accumulator the high order byte of BIGA

   b) Load into the HL pair the address of the high order byte of BIGB

   c) Compare the high order bytes. If they are not equal we are done.
      We have our answer in the sign and overflow flags.

   d) If the high order bytes were equal, repeat comparison on low order
      bytes.

6) To perform HL ← HL − BC:

8080		Z-80	
MOV	A,L	LD	A,L
SUB	C	SUB	C
MOV	L,A	LD	L,A
MOV	A,H	LD	A,H
SBB	B	SBC	A,B
MOV	H,A	LD	H,A

JUMPS, LOOPS AND MODULAR PROGRAMMING

1) For unsigned numbers

	8080		Z-80	
a)	JC	SPOT	JP	C,SPOT
b)	JC	SPOT	JP	C,SPOT
	JZ	SPOT	JP	Z,SPOT

133

By using these two jumps one after the other, both the < case and
the = case are handled.

```
      c)  JZ   SPOT              JP   Z,SPOT

      d)  JNZ  SPOT              JP   NZ,SPOT

      e)  JNC  SPOT              JP   NC,SPOT

      f)  JC   SKIP              JR   C,SKIP

          JZ   SKIP              JR   Z,SKIP

          JMP  SPOT              JP   SPOT

SKIP:   .                 SKIP:   .
        .                         .
        .                         .
```

The method used here is to <u>avoid</u> jumping to SPOT if VARA ≤ VARB.
Other techniques are possible as well.

2) For signed numbers. In several instances here, we will want the
    the effect of (V XOR S), but there is no single instruction that
    will exclusive or flags for us. The following flow chart will
    outline the test we must make:

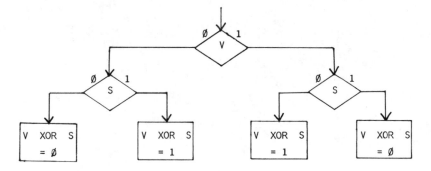

We will use the carry flag to hold the result of (V XOR S).

	8080			Z-80
	STC		(Set the carry)	SCF
	JO	A	(Jump if V = 1)	JP PE,A
	CMC		(Now C = V)	CCF
A:	JP	B	(Jump if S = ∅)	A: JP P,B
	CMC		(Now C = V XOR S)	CCF
B:	NOP		(Do nothing used so B can be a label on an instruction.)	B: NOP

134

At the conclusion of this little sequence of code, the carry flag can be used just as it was used in unsigned numbers. Let's name the above sequence VXORS. (If your assembler has macro capability, look into how you could create a macro named VXORS to perform the above sequence.)

Now the answer to this exercise can be given. Everywhere VXORS is used, it means the above five instructions.

	8Ø8Ø			Z-8Ø	
a)	VXORS			VXORS	
	JC	SPOT		JP	C,SPOT
b)	VXORS			VXORS	
	JC	SPOT		JP	C,SPOT
	JZ	SPOT		JP	Z,SPOT
c)	JZ	SPOT		JP	Z,SPOT
d)	JNZ	SPOT		JP	NZ,SPOT
e)	VXORS			VXORS	
	JNC	SPOT		JP	NC,SPOT
f)	VXORS			VXORS	
	JC	SKIP		JR	C,SKIP
	JZ	SKIP		JR	Z,SKIP
	JMP	SPOT		JP	SPOT
SKIP:	⋮		SKIP:	⋮	

Except for the addition of VXORS, these are identical to the answers to exercise #1.

3) Inputs: ARYADR — start address of the array

   SIZE — number of elements

   Outputs: REGISTER A — Sum (If no overflow)

   OVFLAG — set to a value of 1 if overflow

	8Ø8Ø		
SUM:	PUSH	B	Save BC register pair
	PUSH	H	Save HL register pair
	LHLD	ARYADR	Fetch start address of the array

	SUB	A	Zero the accumulator
	STA	OVFLAG	Clear overflow flag
	LDA	SIZE	Fetch the number of elements
	ANA	A	Checks to see if there are zero elements in the array without changing the value in A
	JZ	DONE	If there are none, we're done. The sum is correctly reported as zero
	MOV	B,A	Otherwise, move the size to register B
	SUB	A	Zero the sum
LOOP:	ADD	M	Add array value
	JNO	OK	Jump if no overflow occurred
	MVI	A,1	Otherwise A ← 1
	STA	OVFLAG	Set the overflow flag
	JMP	DONE	Done
	INX	H	Next element
OK:	DCR	B	Decrement count
	JNZ	LOOP	Repeat until done
DONE:	POP	H	Restore HL pair
	POP	B	Restore BC pair
	RET		

Z-8Ø

SUM:	PUSH	BC	Save BC register pair
	PUSH	HL	Save HL register pair
	LD	HL,(ARYADR)	Fetch start address of the array
	SUB	A	Zero the accumulator
	LD	(OVFLAG),A	Clear the overflow flag
	LD	A,(SIZE)	Fetch the number of elements
	AND	A	Checks to see if there are zero elements in the array without changing the value in A
	JR	Z,DONE	If there are none, we're done. The sum is correctly reported as zero
	LD	B,A	Otherwise, move the size to register B
	SUB	A	Zero the sum
LOOP:	ADD	A,(HL)	Add array value
	JP	PO,OK	Jump if no overflow occurred
	LD	A,1	Otherwise A ← 1
	LD	(OVFLAG),A	Set the overflow flag
	JR	DONE	Done
	INC	HL	Next element
OK:	DJNZ	LOOP	Decrement count
DONE:	POP	HL	Restore HL pair
	POP	BC	Restore BC pair
	RET		

4) Other methods are possible, but this one first compares high order bytes, if equal, then low order bytes.

8Ø8Ø			Z-8Ø	
LHLD	BIGB	(Fetch BIGB)	LD	HL,(BIGB)
LDA	BIGA+1	(Fetch high order byte of BIGA)	LD	A,(BIGA+1)
CMP	H	(Compare high order)	CP	H
JZ	CKLOW	(If equal, check low)	JR	Z,CKLOW
JC	CALB	(A conditional call won't work	JR	C,CALB
JMP	CALA	here. Why?)	JR	CALA
CKLOW: LDA	BIGA	(Fetch low order byte of BIGA)	CKLOW: LD	A,(BIGA)
CMP	L	(Compare low order)	CP	L
JNC	CALA	(Jump if BIGA larger)	JR	NC,CALA
CALB: CALL	BBIGR		CALB: CALL	BBIGR
JMP	DONE	(To avoid calling ABIGR upon return from BBIGR)	JP	DONE
CALA: CALL	ABIGR		CALA: CALL	ABIGR
DONE: ⋮			DONE: ⋮	

5) Simply insert "VXORS" right after the "Compare High Order." Why is it <u>not</u> needed after the "Compare Low Order"?

6) Continued on next page.

8Ø8Ø			Z-8Ø	
LDA	COUNT	(Fetch # of clients; this time we will assume that count ≠ Ø)	LD	A,(COUNT)
MOV	B,A	(Save in register B)	LD	B,A
LXI	H,PEOPLE	(Start address of the array)	LD	HL,PEOPLE
LXI	D,3	(Increment for the address)	LD	DE,3
MVI	A,ØFAH	(FA_H is the desired descriptor byte)	LD	A,ØFAH
LOOP: CMP	M	(Compare to person in Array)	LOOP: CP	(HL)
JZ	MATCH	(Jump if match found)	JR	Z,MATCH
DAD	D	(Increment to next person)	ADD	HL,DE
DCR	B	(Repeat until Match or Done)	DJNZ	LOOP
JNZ	LOOP			
CALL	NOSUCH	(No match found)	CALL	NOSUCH
⋮			⋮	
MATCH: INX	H	(To point to jump address)	MATCH: INC	HL
MOV	E,M	(Fetch low order byte)	LD	E,(HL)

137

INX	H	(To point to high order)	INC	HL	
MOV	D,M	(Fetch high order byte)	LD	D,(HL)	
XCHG		(Jump address in HL)	EX	DE,HL	
PCHL		(Jump)	JP	(HL)	

Match could be included inside the loop by changing the jump on zero to
a jump on non-zero and skipping around this piece of code. The only
reason it's not done that way here is to clearly separate the two
problems:

      a)   looping through PEOPLE looking for a match, and

      b)   transferring to the jump address, when a match is found.

NOTE: A structure such as PEOPLE which contains jump addresses is often
called a vector table. The jump address itself is usually called
a vector.

BIT FIDDLING AND MESSAGE MAKING

1) Input: MLTPLR   two eight bit positive numbers

              MLTCND

   Output: PRODCT   a two byte product of the two inputs

The 8080 version of this subroutine and its Z-80 counterpart will
differ significantly owing to the ability of the Z-80 to rotate
and shift any desired register. The two routines will therefore
be presented separately.

```
         8080      Multiply   Subroutine
MLTPLY:  PUSH      PSW        SAVE REGISTERS
         PUSH      B
         PUSH      D

         LDA       MLTPLR     Fetch multiplier
         MOV       E,A        Save in low order byte of DE pair
         LDA       MLTCND     Fetch multiplicand
         MOV       C,A        Save in register C.
         MVI       B,8        Load the loop counter in B.
         MVI       D,0        Zero high order byte of DE pair
```

138

```
LOOP:      MOV     A,E         To check bit Ø of the multiplier
           RRC                 Shift bit Ø into carry
           JNC     NOADD       If it is zero, skip the addition
           MOV     A,D         If set, add the multiplicand to the
           ADD     C               order byte
           MOV     D,A         Replace the result

NOADD:     MOV     A,D         The apparent redundancy is due to the case
                               where the original move to A from D was
                               skipped
           ANA     A           Clear carry
           RAR                 Shift high order byte
           MOV     D,A         Replace the result
           MOV     A,E         Fetch low order byte
           RAR                 Shift low order byte bringing in bit Ø
                               of the high order byte
           MOV     E,A         Replace low order byte
           DCR     B           Loop increment
           JNZ     LOOP        Repeat until done
           XCHG                Swap DE and HL
           SHLD    PRODCT      The result was in the DE pair
           XCHG                Swap back
           POP     D
           POP     B
           POP     PSW
           RET                 Done
```

	Z-8Ø	Multiply	Subroutine

```
MLIPLY:    PUSH    AF          Save registers
           PUSH    BC
           PUSH    DE
           LD      A,(MLTPLR)  Fetch multiplier
           LD      E,A         Save in low order byte of DE pair
           LD      A,(MLTCND)  Fetch multiplicand
           LD      C,A         Save in register C
           LD      B,8         Load the loop counter in B
           SUB     A           Clear the A register. Registers A and E
                               will be used as a pair during formation
                               of the product
LOOP:      BIT     Ø,E         Check bit Ø of the multiplier
           JR      Z,NOADD     If it is zero, skip the addition
```

```
          ADD      A,C          If set, add the multiplicand to the high
                                order byte
NOADD:    SRL      A            Shift the high order byte right
          RR       E            Shift the low order byte bringing in bit
                                Ø of the high order byte
          DJNZ     LOOP         Repeat until done
          LD       D,A          Place high order byte of product into high
                                order byte of DE pair
          LD       (PRODCT),DE  Store result


          POP      DE           Restore registers
          POP      BC
          POP      AF
          RET                   Done
```

2) Inputs: MLTPLR   Two eight bit numbers not necessarily positive
                MLTCND

           PRODCT   A two byte product of the two inputs

	8Ø8Ø		Comments		Z-8Ø	
MULT2:	PUSH	PSW	Save registers	MULT2:	PUSH	AF
	PUSH	H			PUSH	BC
	PUSH	D			PUSH	DE
	MVI	H,Ø	Clear sign of result flag		LD	B,Ø
	LDA	MLTPLR	Fetch first operand		LD	A,(MLTPLR)
	MOV	E,A	Save in E		LD	E,A
	ANA	A	Test sign of number		AND	A
	JP	POS 1	Skip complement if positive		JP	P,POS 1
	CMA		Form 2's complement if		NEG	
	INR	A	negative			
	INR	H	Increment sign of result flag		INC	B
POS 1:	STA	MLTPLR	Replace positive multiplier	POS 1:	LD	(MLTPLR),A
	LDA	MLTCND	Fetch second operand		LD	A,(MLTCND)
	MOV	D,A	Save in D		LD	D,A
	ANA	A	Test sign of number		AND	A
	JP	POS 2	Skip complement if positive		JP	P,POS 2
	CMA		Form 2's complement if		NEG	
	INR	A	negative			

140

	8080		Comment		Z-80	
	INR	H	Increment sign of result flag		INC	B
POS 2:	STA	MLTCND	Replace positive multiplicand	POS 2:	LD	(MLTCND),A
	CALL	MLTPLY	Get positive result in		CALL	MLTPLY
	MOV	A,H	product		BIT	Ø,B
	RAR		Test bit Ø of sign of result flag			
	JNC	RESPOS	If the bit is Ø the result is positive. Otherwise complement the result		JR	Z,RESPOS
	LHLD	PRODCT	Fetch the result		LD	BC,(PRODCT)
	MOV	A,H	Form 1's complement		LD	A,B
	CMA		of each byte		CPL	
	MOV	H,A			LD	B,A
	MOV	A,L			LD	A,C
	CMA				CPL	
	MOV	L,A			LD	C,A
	INX	H	Increment register pair for 2's complement		INC	BC
	SHLD	PRODCT	Store the properly signed result		LD	(PRODCT),BC
RESPOS:	MOV	A,E	Restore initial signed inputs in MLTPLR and MLTCND	RESPOS:	LD	A,E
	STA	MLTPLR			LD	(MLTPLR),A
	MOV	A,D			LD	A,D
	STA	MLTCND			LD	(MLTCND),A
	POP	D	Restore registers		POP	DE
	POP	H			POP	BC
	POP	PSW			POP	AF
	RET		Done		RET	

3) Inputs: DIVDND – A two byte positive number

   DIVSOR – A one byte positive number

   Outputs: QOTENT – A one byte positive quotient

   RMANDR – A one byte positive remainder or a flag value of –1 on overflow

Again, separate 8080 and Z-80 versions will be given.

8080	Division	Subroutine	
DIVIDE: PUSH	PSW	Save registers	
PUSH	B		
PUSH	D		

```
          LDED    DIVDND      Fetch dividend into the DE register pair
          LDA     DIVSOR      Fetch divisor
          MOV     C,A         Save in register  C
          MVI     B,8         Loop counter in register  B

LOOP:     MOV     A,E         Shift low order byte to the left
          ANA     A           Clear carry
          RAL                 Shift
          MOV     E,A         Replace value
          MOV     A,D         Fetch high order byte
          RAL                 Rotate bringing in high order bit
          SUB     C           Subtract divisor
          JP      SETBIT      If result was positive, jjmp
          ADD     C           Otherwise add back divisor
          MOV     D,A         Replace high order byte
          JMP     NEXT        Go to increment phase
SETBIT:   MOV     D,A         Replace high order byte
          MOV     A,E         Fetch low order byte
          ORI     1           Set low order bit
          MOV     E,A         Replace low order byte
NEXT:     DCR     B           Decrement loop counter
          JNZ     LOOP        Repeat until done
          MOV     A,E         Quotient
          ANA     A           Test sign of result
          JP      OK          If positive, the result is accurate
          MVI     A,-1        Set overflow value
          STA     RMANDR
          JMP     DONE        Jump
OK:       STA     QOTENT      Save quotient
          MOV     A,D         Remainder
          STA     RMANDR      Save remainder

DONE:     POP     D           Restore Registers
          POP     B
          POP     PSW
          RET


          Z-8Ø    Division    Subroutine
DIVIDE:   PUSH    AF          Save registers
          PUSH    BC
          PUSH    DE
```

```
          LD      DE,(DIVDND)  Fetch dividend into the DE register pair
          LD      A,(DIVSOR)   Fetch divisor
          LD      C,A          Save in register  C
          LD      B,8          Loop counter in register  B
          LD      A,D          Will use registers  A  and  E  as a pair
                               during formation of the quotient

LOOP:     SLA     E            Shift low order byte
          RLA                  Rotate high order byte bringing in carry
          SUB     C            Subtract divisor
          JP      P,SETBIT     If the result was positive, jump
          ADD     A,C          Otherwise add back divisor
          JP      NEXT         Go to increment phase
SETBIT:   SET     Ø,E          Set low order bit
NEXT:     DJNZ    LOOP         Repeat until done
          BIT     7,E          Test sign of result
          JR      Z,OK         If positive, the result is accurate
          LD      A,-1         Set overflow flag
          LD      (RMANDR),A
          JR      DONE         Jump
OK:       LD      (RMANDR),A   Save remainder
          LD      A,E          Quotient
          LD      (QOTENT),A   Save quotient
DONE:     POP     DE           Restore registers
          POP     BC
          POP     AF
          RET                  Done
```

4) The purpose of this exercise is to illustrate coding of a routine where
    three pointers must be maintained. Two pointers can be handled easily
    using the DE and HL pairs, but where can a third pointer be stored
    conveniently? The answer is to use the top of the stack. Load the
    first pointer into HL and push it on the stack. Load the second and
    third pointers into the DE and HL register pairs. Now whenever the
    first pointer is needed execute an:

                    XTHL   (8Ø8Ø)

                    EX (SP),HL (Z-8Ø)

    With the above hint, the routine should be within the grasp of the
    reader.

5) Input: WHERE - the address of an array of character
               DIGITS - the number of characters in the array

   Output: RESULT - a two byte binary number equal to the value input
                         in the character string

       e.g.   WHERE   31 30 30 31$_{ASCII}$

               RESULT = 0000 0000 0000 1001

Separate 8080 and Z-80 versions will be given. Both will call a
hypothetical routine named WOOPS if:

   a) the number of characters as recorded in DIGITS
       exceeds 16

   b) any character appears in the array that is neither
       a 31$_H$ or a 30$_H$

	8080	Convert	Binary Input
CBININ:	PUSH	PSW	Save registers
	PUSH	B	
	PUSH	D	
	PUSH	H	
	LDA	DIGITS	Fetch number of characters
	CPI	17	Test for too many
	CNC	WOOPS	If a carry (borrow) does not occur, call WOOPS
	MOV	B,A	Save DIGITS as a counter
	LHLD	WHERE	Set pointer to character array
	LXI	D,0	Clear DE register to use in forming the result
LOOP:	MOV	A,M	Fetch character
	CPI	30H	Is it a "0"?
	JZ	OK	Yes, jump
	CPI	31H	Is it a "1"?
	CNZ	WOOPS	If not, call WOOPS
OK:	RAR		Shift the 0 or 1 into the carry
	MOV	A,E	Fetch low order byte of result
	RAL		Rotate digit into result
	MOV	E,A	Replace low order byte
	MOV	A,D	Fetch high order byte
	RAL		Rotate digit into result
	MOV	D,A	Replace high order byte
	INX	H	Next character
	DCR	B	Decrement count
	JNZ	LOOP	Repeat until done
	XCHG		Swap DE and HL

144

```
        SHLD    RESULT      Store final result
        XCHG                Swap back
        POP     H           Restore registers
        POP     D
        POP     B
        POP     PSW
        RET                 Done


        Z-8Ø    Convert     Binary Input
CBININ: PUSH    AF          Save registers
        PUSH    BC
        PUSH    DE
        PUSH    HL
        LD      A,(DIGITS)  Fetch number of characters
        CP      17          Test for too many
        CALL    NC,WOOPS    If a carry (borrow) does not occur, call WOOPS
        LD      B,A         Save DIGITS as a conter
        LD      HL,(WHERE)  Set pointer to character array
        LD      DE,Ø        Clear DE register to use in forming the result
LOOP:   LD      A,(HL)      Fetch character
        CP      3ØH         Is it a "Ø"?
        JR      Z,OK        Yes, jump
        CP      31H         Is is a "1"?
        CALL    NZ,WOOPS    If not, call WOOPS
OK:     RRA                 Shift the Ø or 1 into the carry
        RL      E           Rotate digit into low order byte
        RL      D           Rotate high order byte
        INC     HL          Next character
        DJNZ    LOOP        Repeat until done
        LD      (RESULT),DE Store final result
        POP     HL          Restore registers
        POP     DE
        POP     BC
        POP     AF
        RET                 Done
```

6) a) When each character input is a hexadecimal digit, you will want
        want to verify that each character in the buffer lies in the range:

$$a) \quad 3\emptyset_H \le Char \le 39_H \quad (\emptyset-9)$$

$$b) \quad 41_H \le Char \le 46_H \quad (A-F)$$

$$c) \quad 61_H \le Char \le 66_H \quad (a-f)$$

145

In range a, you will naturally subtract 30_H.

In range b, a subtraction of 37_H will produce the appropriate hex digit.

In range c, the number to subtract is 57_H.

After the digit has been isolated, it will occupy the order four bits of the accumulator. Shifting those bits into the result should pose no problem.

b) Input: WHERE - the address of the character array
             DIGITS - the number of characters in the array
    Output: RESULT - a two byte value of the number

During the course of the subroutine, it will be necessary to multiply a two byte value by 10. The method to be used will be to multiply the high and low order bytes separately. The two could then be added as:

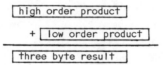

In fact, however, if the high order byte of the high order product is non-zero, it will be time to call WOOPS. The sum would overflow the size of the result.

	8080	Decimal to Binary Input Subroutine	
DECBIN:	PUSH	PSW	Save registers
	PUSH	B	
	PUSH	D	
	PUSH	H	
	LDA	DIGITS	Fetch number of digits
	CPI	6	The largest signed number that will fit is 32,767
	CNC	WOOPS	Call if more than five digits (this still won't guarantee no overflow)
	MOV	B,A	Save count
	LHLD	WHERE	Load address of character array
	LXI	D,0	Clear DE register for the result

146

```
LOOP:   MOV     A,M         Fetch character
        CPI     30H         Is it under 30H?
        CC      WOOPS       Yes, call WOOPS
        SUI     30H         The digit must be OK, subtract
        MOV     C,A         To get its binary value, save in C. We
                            now need to multiply the result already
                            forming by 10.  This will be done in two
                            separate operations.

        MOV     A,E         Fetch low order byte
        STA     MLTCND      Store as multiplicand
        MVI     A,10
        STA     MLTPLR      Store 10 as multiplier
        CALL    MLTPLY      Multiply the.two
        MOV     A,D         Fetch high order byte
        XCHG                Swap DE and HL
        LHLD    PRODCT      Retch result
        XCHG                Swap back
        STA     MLTCND      Store high order as multiplicand
        CALL    MLTPLY      Multiply by same multiplier
        LDA     PRODCT+I    High order byte
        ANA     A           Test for zero
        CNZ     WOOPS       If it isn't, call WOOPS
        LDA     PRODCT      Low order byte
        ADD     D           Add to high order of previous product
        CO      WOOPS       If overflow, call WOOPS

        MOV     D,A         Place result in low order
        MOV     A,C         Fetch new digit
        ADD     E           Add to low order
        MOV     E,A         Replace low order
        MVI     A,0         Clear A without destroying flags
        ADC     D           Add in any carry from low order
        CO      WOOPS       If overflow, call WOOPS
        MOV     D,A         Replace high order
        INX     H           To point to next digit
        DCR     B           Decrement count
        JNZ     LOOP        Repeat until done
        XCHG                Swap DE and HL
        SHLD    RESULT      Store result
        POP     H           Restore registers
        POP     D
        POP     B
        POP     PSW
        RET                 Done
```

	Z-80	Decimal to	Binary Input Subroutine
DECBIN:	PUSH	AF	Save registers
	PUSH	BC	
	PUSH	DE	
	PUSH	HL	
	LD	A,(DIGITS)	Fetch number of digits
	CP	6	The largest signed number that will fit is 32,767
	CALL	NC,WOOPS	Call if more than five digits (this still won't guarantee no overflow.)
	LD	B,A	Save count
	LD	HL,(WHERE)	Load address of character array
	LD	DE,Ø	Clear DE register for the result
LOOP:	LD	A,(HL)	Fetch character
	CP	3ØH	Is it under 3ØH?
	CALL	C,WOOPS	Yes, call WOOPS
	CP	3AH	Is it over 39H?
	CALL	NC,WOOPS	Yes, call WOOPS
	SUB	3ØH	The digit must be OK, subtract
	LD	C,A	to get its binary value, save in C. We now need to multiply the result already forming by 1Ø. This will be done in two separate operations.
	LD	A,E	Fetch low order byte
	LD	(MLTCND),A	Store as multiplicand
	LD	A,1Ø	
	LD	(MLTPLR),A	Store 1Ø as multiplier
	CALL	MLTPLY	Multiply the two
	LD	A,D	Fetch high order byte
	LD	DE,(RESULT)	Fetch result
	LD	(MLTCND),A	Store high order as multiplicand
	CALL	MLTPLY	Multiply by same multiplier
	LD	A,(RESULT+1)	High order byte
	AND	A	Test for zero
	CALL	NZ,WOOPS	If it isn't, call WOOPS
	LD	A,(RESULT)	Low order byte
	ADD	A,D	Add to high order of previous product
	CALL	PE,WOOPS	If overflow, call WOOPS
	LD	D,A	Place result in low order
	LD	C	Fetch new digit
	ADD	A,E	Add to low order
	LD	E,A	Replace low order
	LD	A,Ø	Clear A without destroying flags
	ADC	A,D	Add in any carry from low order

```
CALL    PE,WOOPS    If overflow, call WOOPS
LD      D,A         Replace high order
INC     HL          To point to next digit
DJNZ    LOOP        Decrement Count
                    Repeat until done
LD      (RESULT),DE Store result
POP     HL          Restore registers
POP     DE
POP     BC
POP     AF
RET                 Done
```

7) Translating back from binary to character should pose no problems in
    the case of binary and hexadecimal values. The algorithm for converting
    back from binary into decimal is a little trickier. The trick is to
    divide the two byte value by 1Ø and use the remainder as the <u>lowest</u>
    order digit. Then divide what's left of the result by 1Ø again and
    so on, so that the character value is created from right to left.
    The only problem is that you are very likely to get an overflow on the
    first division. How can you break the division into two pieces to
    get around this problem?

A CASUAL INTRODUCTION TO DATA STRUCTURES

1) Due to the machine dependent aspects of I/O, it is not possible to
    present a routine that is guaranteed to work on your system. The
    routine called KYBDIN that accepts a single character from the
    keyboard and leaves its value in the accumulator. Echoing is
    accomplished by calling a hypothetical routine called VIDOUT which
    accepts a single character in the accumulator and displays it on
    the screen. It is assumed that this routine does not destroy the
    contents of the accumulator.

```
8Ø8Ø      String    Input    Routine
BUFFER:   .BLKB     3Ø       Reserve 3Ø bytes of storage
STRGIN:   PUSH      PSW      Save registers
          PUSH      B
          PUSH      H
          LXI       H,BUFFER Set HL to point to the buffer
          MVI       A,2ØH    ASCII for a space
          MVI       B,3Ø     Number of characters in buffer
CLRLOP:   MOV       M,A      Clear buffer location
          INX       H        Next buffer location
```

149

```
          DCR     B           Decrement count
          JNZ     CLRLOP      Repeat until entire buffer cleared
          LXI     H,BUFFER    Reset pointer to start of buffer
          MVI     B,30        Overflow counter
INLOOP:   CALL    KYBDIN      Get character
          CALL    VIDOUT      Echo
          CPI     0DH         Carriage return?
          JZ      DONE        Yes, jump out of loop
          MOV     M,A         Else, store in buffer
          INX     H           Next buffer location
          DCR     B           Overflow counter
          JNZ     INLOOP      Repeat if not full
DONE:     POP     H           Restore registers
          POP     B
          POP     PSW
          RET                 Done
```

Z-80	String	Input	Routine

```
BUFFER:   .BLKB   30          Reserve 30 bytes of storage
STRGIN:   PUSH    AF          Save registers
          PUSH    BC
          PUSH    DE
          PUSH    HL
          LD      A,20H       ASCII for a space
          LD      (BUFFER),A  Clear first character
          LD      HL,BUFFER   Pointer to first character
          LD      DE,BUFFER+1     Pointer to second character
          LD      BC,29       Number of characters to be cleared
          LDIR                Clear buffer
          LD      B,30        Overflow counter
INLOOP:   CALL    KYBDIN      Get character
          CALL    VIDOUT      Echo
          CO      0DH         Carriage return?
          JR      Z,DONE      Yes, jump out of loop
          LD      (HL),A      Otherwise, store character
          INC     HL          Next buffer location
          DJNZ    INLOOP      Repeat until full or carriage return
DONE:     POP     HL          Restore registers
          POP     DE
          POP     BC
          POP     AF
          RET                 Done
```

2) See note to exercise #1. The subroutine below uses VIDOUT.

INPUT: WHERE – start address of the buffer

COUNT – number of characters

8Ø8Ø	String	Output	Routine
STROUT:	PUSH	PSW	Save registers
	PUSH	B	
	PUSH	H	
	LHLD	WHERE	Fetch start address
	LDA	COUNT	Fetch number of characters
	MOV	B,A	Save count
OUTLOP:	MOV	A,M	Fetch character
	CALL	VIDOUT	Output to screen
	INX	H	Next character
	DCR	B	Decrement count
	JNZ	OUTLOP	Repeat until done
	POP	H	Restore registers
	POP	B	
	POP	PSW	
	RET		Done

Z-8Ø	String	Output	Routine
STROUT:	PUSH	AF	Save registers
	PUSH	BC	
	PUSH	HL	
	LD	HL,(WHERE)	Fetch start address
	LD	A,(COUNT)	Fetch number of characters
	LD	B,A	Save count
OUTLOP:	LD	A,(HL)	Fetch character
	CALL	VIDOUT	Output to screen
	INC	HL	Next character
	DJNZ	OUTLOP	Decrement count, repeat until done
	POP	HL	Restore registers
	POP	BC	
	POP	AF	
	RET		Done

3) The driver will be a simple matter of moving data and calling STROUT and STRGIN _if_ the data is structured carefully. When you know in

advance the exact message you want output, define it in ASCII in
your data area. Count up the length and store it as a constant as
well. The driver routine will be trivial if the data is defined as
follows (use the keywords your assembler wants to see):

```
MSG1:    .ASCII     "Name?"
MSG2:    .ASCII     "Address?"
MSG3:    .ASCII     "Phone number?"
LEN1     .BYTE      5
LEN2     .BYTE      8
LEN3     .BYTE      13
NAME:    .BLKB      20
ADDRSS:  .BLKB      30
PHONE:   .BLKB      8   (the extra character is for the   "-")
```

4) The storage area can be reserved using:

```
           .LOC      2000  (or some page boundry address)
POOL:      .BLKB     400H
```

a)   8080   Link-up   Subroutine

```
LINKUP: PUSH     PSW
        PUSH     B        Save registers
        PUSH     D
        PUSH     H
        LXI      H,POOL       Start address of space
        SHLD     AVAIL        Avail will point to first node
        LXI      D,POOL+64    DE will point to next node
        LXI      B,127        BC=(node size*2) -1 (the reason should become clear later
        MVI      A,15         The number of nodes that will fit minus 1.
SETLOP: MOV      M,E          Low order byte of link
        INX      H            Point to next byte
        MOV      M,D          High order byte of link
        DAD      B            To point to the node after next
        XCHG                  Now HL points to the next node
        DCR      A            Decrement loop counter
        JNZ      SETLOP       Repeat until all nodes have link fields set but the last
        MOV      M,A          Set final link value of all 0's
        INX      H
        MOV      M,A
        POP      H            Retore registers
        POP      D
```

152

```
        POP     B
        POP     PSW
        RET             Done


        Z-80    Link-up Subroutine
LINKUP: PUSH    AF
        PUSH    BC      Save registers
        PUSH    DE
        PUSH    HL
        LD      HL,POOL     Start address of space
        LD      (AVAIL),HL  Avail will point to first node
        LD      DE,POOL+64  DE will point to next node
        LD      BC,127      BC=(node size*2) -1 (the reason should become clear later)
        LD      A,15        The number of nodes that will fit minus 1
SETLOP: LD      (HL),E      Low order byte of link
        INC     HL          Point to next byte
        LD      (HL),D      High order byte of link
        ADD     HL,BC       To point to the node after next
        EX      DE,HL       Now HL points to the next node
        DEC     A           Decrement loop counter
        JR      NZ,SETLOP   Repeat until all nodes have link fields set but the last
        LD      (HL),A      Set final link value of all Ø's
        INC     HL
        LD      (HL),A
        POP     HL      Restore registers
        POP     DE
        POP     BC
        POP     AF
        RET             Done


b)      8Ø8Ø    Get-node Subroutine
GETNOD: PUSH    PSW     Save registers
        PUSH    D
        LHLD    AVAIL   Fetch pointer to next available node
        MOV     A,L     Test for all zeroes which would indicate no more
        ORA     H       nodes available
        CZ      OVFLOW  Call hypothetical overflow routine if no nodes are left
        MOV     E,M     Otherwise fetch link field from this node
        INX     H
        MOV     D,M
        XCHG            Swap DE + HL
        SHLD    AVAIL   Set new pointer in avail
```

153

XCHG		Swap back so HL points to new node
POP	D	Restore registers
POP	PSW	
RET		Done

Z-8Ø	Get-node	Subroutine
GETNOD: PUSH	AF	Save registers
PUSH	DE	
LD	HL,(AVAIL)	Fetch pointer to next available node
LD	A,L	Test for all Ø's which would indicate no more nodes
OR	H	available
CALL	Z,OVFLOW	Call hypothetical overflow routine if no nodes are left
LD	E,(HL)	Otherwise fetch link field from this node
INC	HL	
LD	D,(HL)	
LD	(AVAIL),DE	Set new pointer in avail
POP	DE	Restore registers
POP	AF	
RET		Done

c) Since there are no overflow worries, this routine should pose no problems. A basic attack might involve:
1) fetch value of avail (pointer to next node on avail list)
2) store that pointer in link field of node to be returned
3) store pointer to returned node in avail

BINARY CODED DECIMAL ARITHMETIC

1) The method to be used involves two separate subroutines. The first subroutine will accept a pointer to a buffer which contains only digits in character form and will translate from left to right into BCD. The second subroutine will analyze the original raw input extracting punctuation and stray characters. It will then call the first and pass it the byte count and address in register B and the DE register pair respectively. The final BCD number will be placed in an array called NUMBER. The first three bytes of NUMBER will be its descriptor block.

8Ø8Ø	Digit	to BCD Subroutine
DGTBCD: PUSH	PSW	Save registers
PUSH	B	
PUSH	D	

154

```
           PUSH    H
           LXI     H,NUMBER+3    First destination slot for BCD output
LOOP:      LDAX    D             Fetch digit
           SUI     30H           Delete ASCII code
           RAL                   Rotate four times to the left
           RAL
           RAL
           RAL
           MOV     C,A           Save
           INX     D             Point to next digit
           LDAX    D             Fetch next digit
           SUI     30H           Delete ASCII code
           ADD     C             To form BCD pair of digits
           MOV     M,A           Save in number
           INX     D             Next digit
           INX     H             Next byte in number
           DCR     B             Decrement byte count
           JNZ     LOOP          Repeat until done
           POP     H             Restore registers
           POP     D
           POP     B
           POP     PSW
           RET                   Done
```

Z-80   Digit to BCD Subroutine

Unlike the 8080 version. This subroutine affects the contents
of the buffer location passed to it.

```
DGTBCD:   PUSH    AF            Save registers
          PUSH    BC
          PUSH    DE
          PUSH    HL
          LD      HL,NUMBER+3   Pointer to output area
          SUB     A             Clear accumulator
LOOP:     EX      DE,HL         Swap pointers so HL points to input buffer
          RRD                   Bring in binary form of first digit
          LD      (DE),A        Store in number
          INC     HL            Next character
          RRD                   Bring in binary form
          EX      DE,HL         Swap pointers to HL points to number
          RLD                   Rotate second digit into number
          INC     HL            Next byte
```

155

```
        INC    DE              Next digit
        DJNZ   LOOP            Repeat until done
        POP    HL              Restore registers
        POP    DE
        POP    BC
        POP    AF
        RET                    Done
```

The second subroutine deals with data areas defined as on page 143.
The sizes of BUFFER and NUMBER can be assumed to have been defined
to be large enough to accomodate any number the routine will have
to deal with. That is, the routine needn't do any overflow error
checking. We will also assume that the entire data area for NUMBER
was previously cleared.

```
        8Ø8Ø     Characters to Digits Subroutine
CARTDG: PUSH   PSW
        PUSH   B
        PUSH   D
        PUSH   H
        SUB    A               Clear accumulator
        STA    SPRFLG          Clear spare flag
        LXI    H,BUFFER        Pointer to Buffer + Ø
        LXI    D,BUFFER        Same
PRESIG: LDAX   D               Fetch character
        CPI    2ØH             Is it a space?
        JZ     INCR            Yes, jump
        CPI    24H             Is it a "$"?
        JZ     INCR            Yes, jump
        CPI    2BH             Is it a "+"?
        JZ     INCR            Yes, jump
        CPI    2DH             Is it a "-"?
        JNZ    NOMNUS          No, jump
        MVI    A,-1            Set negative indicator
        STA    NUMBER+2        Place in sign byte
        JMP    INCR            Jump
NOMNUS: CPI    2EH             Is it a "."?
        JNZ    NOPERD          No, jump
        INX    D               Next character
        JMP    POSTDC          Jump
```

156

```
NOPERD: CPI     30H              Is it less than a digit?
        JC      TERMSG           Yes, jump
        CPI     3AH              Is it greater than a digit?
        JNC     TERMSG           Yes, jump
        MOV     M,A              Store character
        INX     D                Increment buffer pointers
        INX     H
        INX     B                Increment digit count
        JMP     POSTSG           Jump
INCR:   INX     D                Next character
        JMP     PRESIG           Repeat

        etc.
```

So the whole routine is just a straightforward coding of the algorithm on pages 143-146. NOTE: Do not call DGTBCD when the number is zero bytes long.

Z-80   Characters to Digits Subroutine

```
CARTDG: PUSH    AF
        PUSH    BC
        PUSH    DE
        PUSH    HL
        SUB     A                Clear accumulator
        LD      (SPRFLG),A       Clear spare flag
        LD      HL,BUFFER        Pointer to Buffer + 0
        LD      DE,BUFFER        Same
PRESIG: LD      A,(DE)           Fetch character
        CP      20H              Is it a space?
        JR      Z,INCR           Yes, jump
        CP      24H              Is is a "$"?
        JR      Z,INCR           Yes, jump
        CP      2BH              Is it a "+"?
        JR      Z,INCR           Yes, jump
        CP      2DH              Is it a "-"?
        JR      NZ,NOMNUS        No, jump
        LD      A,-1             Set negative indicator
        LD      (NUMBER+2),A     Place in sign byte
        JR      INCR             Jump
NOMNUS: CP      2EH              Is it a "."?
        JR      NZ,NOPERD        No, jump
        INX     D                Next character
        JP      POSTDC           Jump
```

157

```
NOPERD:  CP    30H                Is it less than a digit?
         JP    C,TERMSG           Yes, jump
         CP    3AH                Is it greater than a digit?
         JP    NC,TERMSG          Yes, jump
         LD    (HL),A             Store character
         INC   DE                 Increment buffer pointers
         INC   HL
         INC   B                  Increment digit count
         JP    POSTSG             Jump
INCR:    INC   DE                 Next character
         JR    PRESIG             Repeat

         etc.
```

So the whole routine is just a straightforward coding of the algorithm on pages 143-146. NOTE: Do not call DGTBCD when the number is zero bytes long.

2) Fixed point addition:

```
        INPUT:   VARA    -  are two BCD numbers
                 VARB

                 SZMAX   -  number of bytes of storage reserved for each
                            number input
        OUTPUT:  SUM     -  data area where result will be stored or flag
                            result of negative zero on overflow
```

	8080	Fixed Point Addition
SUM:	.BLKB	258	(for max of 256 byte number and 3 byte descriptor block)

```
SUM:     .BLKB  258               (for max of 256 byte number and 3 byte descriptor block)
ENDSUM: .BLKB   1
BLOCKA: .BLKB   3                 (storage area for descriptor blocks of input)
BLOCKB: .BLKB   3
FXPTAD: PUSH    PSW               Save registers
        PUSH    B
        PUSH    D
        PUSH    H
        LXI     D,BLOCKA          Pointer to block save area
        LXI     H,VARA            Pointer to descriptive block
        MVI     B,3               Number of bytes in block
FXPT05: MOV     A,M               Transfer block to block save area
        STAX    D
        INX     H
        INX     D
```

158

```
              DCR      B
              JNZ      FXPT05
              MVI      B,3             Bytes in second block
              LXI      H,VARB          Pointer to second descriptive block (DE already points
                                       to second save area)
FXPT10:  MOV      A,M             Transfer second block to save area
              STAX     D
              INX      H
              INX      D
              DCR      B
              JNZ      FXPT10
              LDA      SZMAX           Fetch maximum size
              MOV      C,A             Save

              (ALIGN DECIMAL POINT)
              LDA      VARB+1          Number of decimal places in VARB
              MOV      B,A             Save
              LDA      VARA+1          Number of decimal places in VARA
              SUB      B               Find the difference
              MOV      D,A             Save
              JZ       FXPT30          Jump if same number of places
              JNC      FXPT25          Jump if  A  has more
              LXI      H,VARA          Pointer to size of VARA
FXPT15:  ADD      M               Get new size
              CMP      C               Compare to maximum size
              JZ       FXPT20          If same, we're OK
              CNC      OVFLOW          If over max, call overflow
FXPT20:  MOV      M,A             Store new size
              MOV      A,D             Restore difference
              INX      H               Pointer to decimal places in variable
              ADD      M               New decimal places
              MOV      M,A             Store new decimal places
              STA      SUM+1           Store decimal places in sum
              JMP      FXPT30          Jump
FXPT25:  LXI      H,VARB          Pointer to size of VARB
              JMP      FXPT15          Get new size

              (CHECK SIGN OF NUMBERS)
FXPT30:  LDA      VARB+2          Sign of VARB
              MOV      B,A             Save
              LDA      VARA+2          Sign of VARA
              CMP      B               Do signs match?
              JNZ      FXPT35          No, jump
              STA      SUM+2           Give their common sign to the result
```

```
            LXI       H,VARA        Pass the parameters to BCD ADD
            SHLD      ADD1
            LXI       H,VARB
            SHLD      ADD2
            LXI       H,SUM
            SHLD      RESULT
            CALL      BCDADD        Add the two numbers
            JMP       FXPT55
FXPT35:     LDA       VARB          Size of VARB
            MOV       B,A           Save
            LDA       VARA          Size of VARA
            CMP       B             Are numbers the same size?
            JNZ       FXPT45        No, jump
            LXI       D,VARA+3      First byte of number of VARA
            LXI       H,VARB+3      First byte of number of VARB
FXPT4Ø:     LDAX      D             Fetch byte of VARA
            CMP       M             Compare to VARB, same?
            JNZ       FXPT45        No, jump
            INX       D             Yes, then check next byte
            INX       H
            DCR       B
            JNZ       FXPT4Ø        Repeat while bytes remain
            SUB       A             The two numbers are equal, so move zero to sum
            STA       SUM
            STA       SUM+1
            STA       SUM+2
            JMP       FXPT55
FXPT45:     JC        FXPT5Ø        Jump if VARB is larger
            LDA       VARA+2
            STA       SUM+2
            LXI       H,VARA        Prepare parameters to subtract VARB from VARA
            SHLD      NMUEND
            LXI       H,VARB
            SHLD      SBTRHD
            LXI       H,SUM
            SHLD      DFFRNC
            CALL      BCDSUB        Subtract
            JMP       FXPT55
FXPT5Ø:     LDA       VARBT2
            STA       SUM+2
            LXI       H,VARB        Prepare parameters to subtract VARA from VARB
            SHLD      MNUEND
            LXI       H,VARA
            SHLD      SBTRHD
            LXI       H,SUM
            SHLD      DFFRNC
```

160

```
FXPT55:  CALL    BCDSUB        The routine is essentially complete.  Just
         .                     move the descriptive blocks back from the save
         .                     area, pop the registers, and return.
         .
```

	Z-80	Fixed Point Addition

SUM:	.BLKB	258	(for max of 256 byte number and 3 byte descriptor block)
ENDSUM:	.BLKB	1	
BLOCKA:		3	(storage area for descriptor blocks of input)
BLOCKB:		3	
FXPTAD:	PUSH	AF	Save registers
	PUSH	BC	
	PUSH	DE	
	PUSH	HL	
	LD	DE,BLOCKA	Pointer to block save area
	LD	HL, VARA	Pointer to descriptive block
	LD	BC,3	Number of bytes in block
	LDIR		Transfer block to block save area
	LD	BC,3	Bytes in second block
	LD	HL,VARB	Pointer to second descriptive block (DE already points to second save area)
	LDIR		Transfer second block to save area
	LD	A,(SZMAX)	Fetch maximum size
	LD	C,A	Save
	(ALIGN DECIMAL POINT)		
	LD	A,(VARB+1)	Number of decimal places in VARB
	LD	B,A	Save
	LD	A,(VARA+1)	Number of decimal places in VARA
	SUB	B	Find the difference
	LD	D,A	Save
	JR	Z,FXPT20	Jump if same number of places
	JP	NC,FXPT15	Jump if A has more
	LD	H,VARA	Pointer to size of VARA
FXPT05:	ADD	A,(HL)	Get new size
	CP	C	Compare to maximum size
	JR	Z,FXPT10	If same, we're OK
	CALL	NC,OVFLOW	If over max, call overflow
FXPT10:	LD	(HL),A	Store new size
	LD	A,D	Restore difference
	INC	HL	Pointer to decimal places in variable
	ADD	A,(HL)	New decimal places
	LD	(HL),A	Store new decimal places

161

```
            LD      (SUM+1),A       Store decimal places in sum
            JP      FXPT20          Jump
FXPT15: LD      HL,VARB         Pointer to size of VARB
            JP      FXPT05          Get new size
            (CHECK SIGN OF NUMBERS)
FXPT20: LD      A,(VARB+2)      Sign of VARB
            LD      B,A             Save
            LD      A,(VARA+2)      ·Sign of VARA
            CP      B               Do sings match?
            JR      NZ,FXPT25       No, jump
            LD      (SUM+2),A       Give their common sign to the result
            LD      HL, VARA        Pass the parameters to BCD ADD
            LD      (ADD1),HL
            LD      HL,VARA
            LD      (ADD2),HL
            LD      HL,SUM
            LD      (RESULT),HL
            CALL    BCDADD          Add the two numbers
            JP      FXPT45
FXPT25: LD      A,(VARB)        Size of VARB
            LD      B,A             Save
            LD      A,(VARA)        Size of VARA
            CP      B               Are numbers the same size?
            JR      NZ,FXPT35       No, jump
            LD      DE,VARA+3       First byte of number of VARA
            LD      HL,VARB+3       First byte of number of VARB
FXPT30: LD      A,(DE)          Fetch byte of VARA
            CP      (HL)            Compare to VARB, same?
            JR      NZ,FXPT35       No, jump
            INC     DE              Yes, then check next byte
            INC     HL
            DJNZ    FXPT30
            SUB     A               The two numbers are equal, so move zero to sum
            LD      (SUM),A
            LD      (SUM+1),A
            LD      (SUM+2),A
            JR      FXPT45
FXPT35: JP      C,FXPT40        Jump if VARB is larger
            LD      A,(VARA+2)
            LD      (SUM+2),A
            LD      HL,VARA         Prepare parameters to subtract VARB from VARA
            LD      (MNUEND),HL
            LD      HL,VARA
```

162

```
          LD        (SBTRHD),HL
          LD        HL,SUM
          LD        (DFFRNC),HL
          CALL      BCDSUB        Subtract
          JR        FXPT45
FXPT40:   LD        A,(VARB+2)
          LD        (SUM+2),A
          LD        HL,VARB       Prepare parameters to subtract VARA from VARB
          LD        (MNUEND),HL
          LD        HL,VARA
          LD        (SBTRHD),HL
          LD        HL,SUM
          LD        (DFFRNC),HL
          CALL      BCDSUB
FXPT45:   .                       Tho routine is essentially complele.  Just move the
          .                       descriptive blocks back from the save area, pop the
          .                       registers, and return.
```

The two routines BCDADD and BCDSUB are extremely simple. They are just
multibyte addition and subtraction with decimal adjust between each add
or subtract. BCDSUB should squeeze out any leading 00 bytes before returning.

3) The fixed point subtract is trivial once the fixed point add has been
    written. The algorithm follows:
        a) load and save the sign of the subtrahend
        b) reverse the sign in the descriptor block
        c) call FXPTAD
        d) replace the original sign

4) A portion of the floating point multiply subroutine will be given here.
    What will not be shown is:
        a) initially saving the registers and the descriptor blocks of
            MLTPLR and MLTCND and clearing PRODCT.
        b) adding the two numbers of digits to the right of the decimal
            point and storing it in the descriptor block of the result
        c) dotormining which number is longer. Placing a pointer to the
            end of the shorter in the HL register pair placing the size of
            the shorter in the C register
        d) determining the sign of the result and storing it
        e) restoring registers and descriptor blocks

    What will be shown is performing the multiplication itself using calls
    to BCDADD.

                                163

```
FPMULT:    .
           .
           .
           XCHG                       Swap DE and HL
           LXI     H,MLTCND           Set up parameters for BCDADD
           SHLD    ADD1
           LXI     H,PRODCT
           SHLD    ADD2
           SHLD    RESULT             i.e., ADD2←ADD1 + ADD2
           XCHG                       Swap back
BIGLP:     MOV     A,M                Fetch byte of multiplier
           ANI     ØFH                Clear high order digit
           JZ      LILP2A
           MOV     B,A                Save as counter
LILP1:     CALL    BCDADD             Add multiplicand a single time
           DCR     B                  Decrement counter
           JNZ     LILP1              Repeat addition the number of times of the digit
LILP2A:    CALL    LFTSFT             Shift number 4 bits to left for multiply by 1Ø
           MOV     A,M                Get byte again
           ANI     ØFØH               Clear low order digit
           JZ      LILP4
           RRC                        Rotate four times
           RRC
           RRC
           RRC
           MOV     B,A                Save as counter
LILP3:     CALL    BCDADD             Add multiplicand a single time
           DCR     B                  Decrement counter
           JNZ     LILP2              Repeat addition the number of times of the digit
LILP4:     CALL    RGTSFT             Shifts the number 4 bits to the right (i.e., back
                                      to original alignment) and adds a ØØ byte to the
                                      end.  This accomplishes a second 4 bit shift to
                                      the left without having the number move through
                                      memory by more than one byte.
           DCX     H                  Next byte of multiplier
           DCR     C                  Decrement byte count
           JNZ     BIGLP              Repeat until done
           .
           .
           .
```

```
FPMULT:    .
           .
           .
           SUB     A                  Clear accumulator
```

```
            LD      HL,MLTCND       Set up parameters for BCDADD
            LD      (ADD1),HL
            LD      HL,PRODCT
            LD      (ADD2),HL
            LD      (RESULT),HL     i.e., ADD2←ADD2 + ADD1
BIGLP:      RRD                     Fetch first digit
            LD      B,A             Save as counter
LILP1:      CALL    BCDADD          Add multiplicand
            DJNZ    LILP1           Repeat the number of times of the digit
            CALL    LFTSFT          Shift number 4 bits to left for multiply by 10
            RRD                     Fetch second digit
            LD      B,A             Save as counter
LILP2:      CALL    BCDADD          Add multiplicand
            DJNZ    LILP2           Repeat the number of times ot the digit
            CALL    RGTSFT          Shifts the number 4 bits to the right (i.e., back
                                    to original alignment) and adds a 00 byte to the
                                    end.  This accomplishes a second 4 bit shift to
                                    the left without having the number move through
                                    memory by more than one byte
            INC     HL              Next byte of multiplier
            DEC     C               Decrement byte count
            JR      NZ,BIGLP        Repeat until done
            :
            .
            o
```

5) Flcating point division will again make use of LFTSFT and RGTSFT to
   prevent the dividend from wandering through memory. It will also save
   and later restore the descriptor blocks of the dividend and divisor.
   It will have to call the fixed point subtract subroutine rather than
   BCDSUB, because the sign of the result is not known beforehand.

index